Delicious Bread Machine Challah

Yield: 2 large challahs

Ingredients:
1¼ cups water or soy milk
3 extra-large eggs
⅓ cup oil
½ cup sugar
1½ Tbsp salt
2 cups whole wheat flour
3½ cups white flour
2½ tsp bread machine yeast

Directions:
Place all ingredients into bread machine in order. Set for dough cycle. (My machine's dough cycle is 2 hours, but I let the dough rise another hour until it's pushing the top of the machine up.)
Turn out dough onto floured and/or sprayed counter. Knead gently for 1 minute.
Shape and braid challahs.
Place on parchment paper-lined baking sheets. Let rise, covered, for 1 hour.
Preheat oven to 350°F. Bake for approximately 20 minutes.

I love this salad, which I adapted from a cookbook. It's festive and tasty without being too different, so even my kids will eat it.

Teriyaki Mushroom Salad

Ingredients:
Salad:
10 oz baby bella mushrooms, quartered
1 Tbsp olive oil
⅓ cup teriyaki sauce
Romaine lettuce
Grape tomatoes
Candied pecans (for a kick, you can use spicy candied pecans instead)

Dressing:
½ cup oil
¼ cup sugar
¼ cup vinegar
¼ cup ketchup
1 garlic clove, crushed, or 1 frozen garlic cube
½ tsp paprika
½ tsp salt
½ tsp mustard (dried or regular)

Directions:
In a small pot, sauté mushrooms in olive oil for a few minutes. Add teriyaki sauce and simmer for about 5 minutes. Remove from flame and cool. Refrigerate until ready to use.
In a container, combine all dressing ingredients. Shake well to emulsify and refrigerate (keeps well in the fridge for months!).
Place lettuce and tomatoes In a bowl. Top with sautéed mushrooms (you may want to take them out of the fridge in advance if olive oil has solidified in the fridge). Add candied nuts and toss with dressing.

⅓ cup brown sugar
1 tsp vanilla sugar
1 cup whole wheat flour
1 tsp baking soda
4½ cups old-fashioned oats

Directions:
Preheat oven to 350°F.
Mix oil, honey, and brown sugar together vigorously. Add vanilla sugar, flour, baking soda, and oats. Press into a 9x13-inch pan and bake for 25 minutes. Slice when still warm.

Just-Perfect Cobbler

Ingredients:
3–4 apples
1 can blueberry pie filling
3 cups flour
1¼ cups sugar
1 egg
1 tsp vanilla sugar
¾ cup oil
1 tsp baking powder

Directions:
Peel and slice apples thinly. Mix with pie filling and spread on bottom of a 9-inch round pan.
Mix together the rest of the ingredients until crumbly. Sprinkle over apple layer.
Bake uncovered at 350°F for 1 hour.

taste

THE BEST OF THE FOOD WORLD

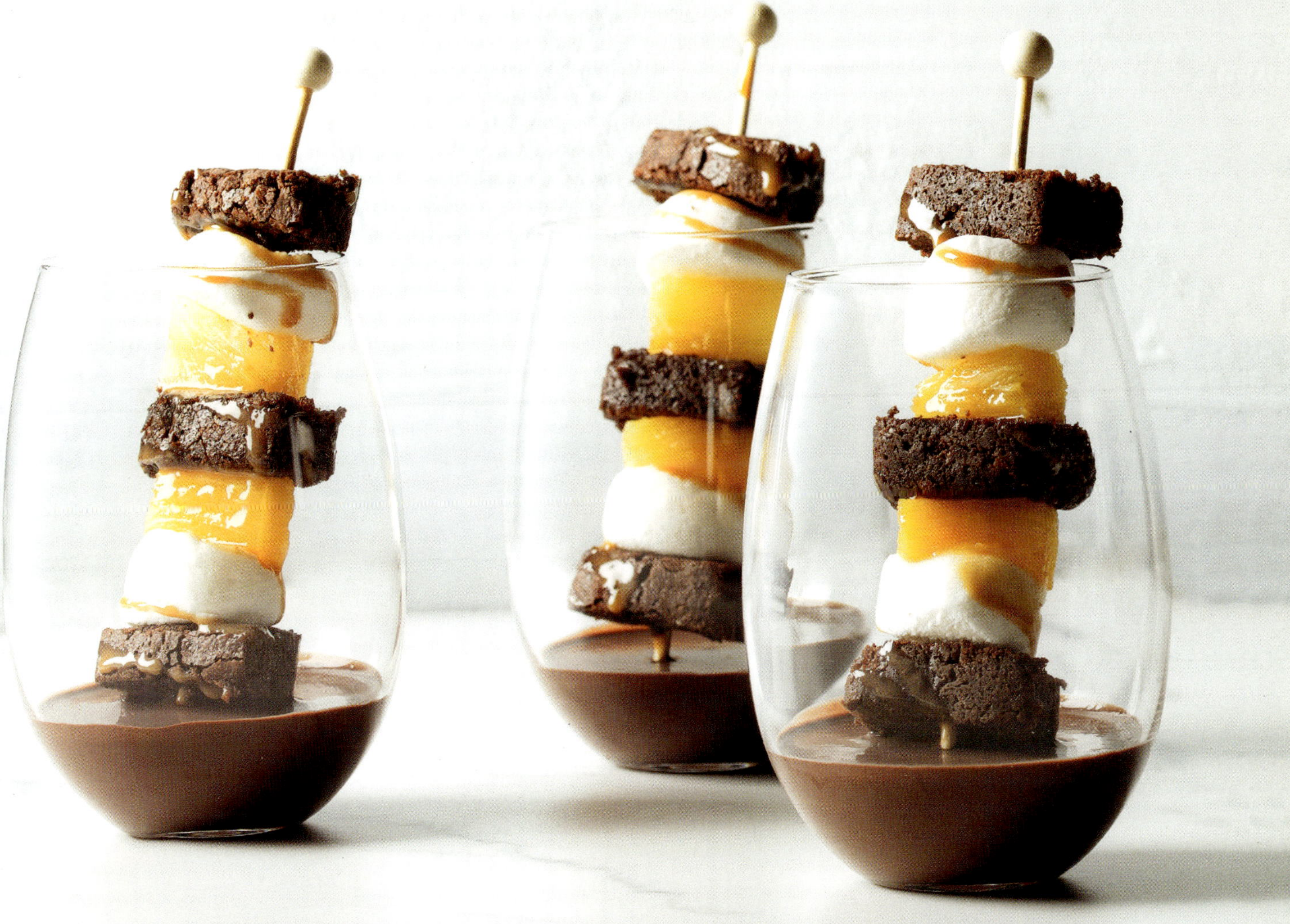

A CURATED COLLECTION OF EVERYDAY AND CONTEMPORARY RECIPES WITH A TWIST

THE VOICE OF LAKEWOOD

DISTRIBUTED BY FELDHEIM

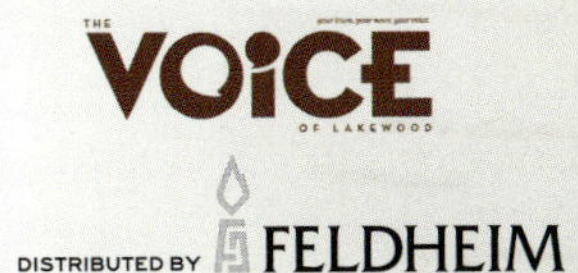

ISBN 978-1-68025-169-2

Coordinated by Aura Dweck
Prepared for print by Malka Selengut
Edited by Shira Hoffman
Poems written by Elky Handler
Book and cover design by Perel Leah Levitin

Distributed by:
Feldheim Publishers
POB 43163 / Jerusalem, Israel
208 Airport Executive Park
Nanuet, NY 10954

www.feldheim.com

Kitchens

If kitchens would have choices,

Then mine would choose its goal:

To nurture, feed,

And fill the need

Of body and of soul.

If kitchens could feel joyous,

Then mine would swell with pride,

As spills and tears

And hidden fears

Are gently wiped inside.

If kitchens would have voices,

Then mine would sing a song

Of tanks refilled

And hearts rebuilt

And I would sing along.

Table of Contents

Starters and Sides

Soups

Salads

Drinks and Pops

Dairy

Fish

Chicken

Healthy Eats

Yamim Tovim

Rosh Hashanah

Sukkos

Chanukah

Tu B'Shevat

Purim

Pesach

Shavuos

About

VOICE

OF LAKEWOOD

Founded in 2005, *The Voice of Lakewood* has been keeping the pulse of the ever-expanding Lakewood community and its environs Jackson, Howell, and Toms River. What began as a monthly magazine quickly morphed into a weekly, with high-quality and entertaining content for the entire family.

In 2016 *The Voice* launched Taste, a premier food section. Taste was new terrain for a free weekly publication, and our food editors and contributors took the reins to provide our readership with recipes that they'd actually eat and enjoy. We take pride in our simple, good food with a presentation that excites yet doesn't overwhelm. We've grown together with Lakewood, and now with the launch of the *Taste* cookbook, we hope our food will be enjoyed by families the world over.

Meet the Taste Contributors

Chay Berger

FOOD PHOTOGRAPHER

I love bringing readers beautiful pictures of wonderful recipes. It's such a great feeling when the shot is finally captured, highlighting the look of the delicious food coming to your table soon.

Dinah Bucholz

RECIPE DEVELOPER

I'm a cookbook author and food columnist. I live in Philadelphia with my family.

Mirel Freylich

RECIPE DEVELOPER AND PHOTOGRAPHER

I love working in the kitchen; my specialty is creating recipes that don't take too long to make. I especially enjoy the art of styling and photographing the different foods I make, bringing the food from my table to yours.

Fun fact:

No matter how short on time I am, I prefer fresh over fancy. I'll prepare the simplest fresh supper rather than eating a more elaborate one from the freezer.

Gitty Friedman

RECIPE DEVELOPER

I love cooking and baking, and my favorite part is watching my family and friends enjoy the food I make. I run a home-based bakery business called The Last Crumb which caters to the Lakewood area.

Fun fact:

I didn't know the first thing about cooking before I got married and I was very worried about how I would manage it!

Sara Goldstein

RECIPE DEVELOPER

I'm a certified chef who trained in classic French and Middle Eastern cuisine at the Jerusalem Culinary Institute. My background includes recipe development, styling, and photography for an array of clients. I specialize in creating easy-to-make, beautiful-to-look-at food.

Fun fact:

Although I absolutely love to bake pastries and bread, I hardly have a sweet tooth. My favorite things to eat are real foods like steak and chicken on the bone.

Naomi Hazan

RECIPE DEVELOPER

I'm a self-taught chef and food columnist based in Brooklyn, NY. My passion is everything food related; I love teaching people how simple and delicious home cooking can be.

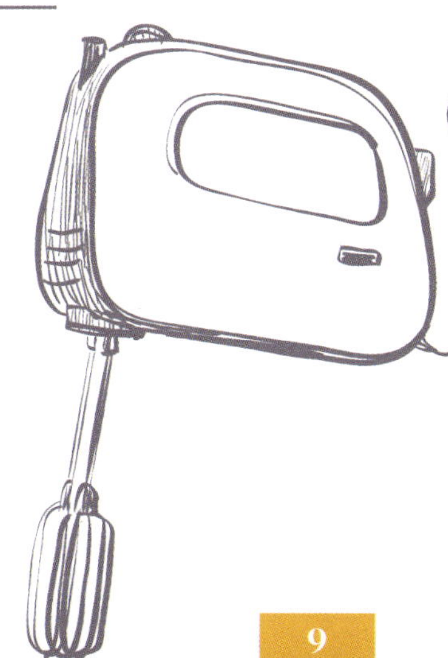

Chana Rivky Klein

FOOD PHOTOGRAPHER

I'm a food stylist and photographer based in New Jersey. As a creative, styling is my passion; it's what drew me to this field in the first place.

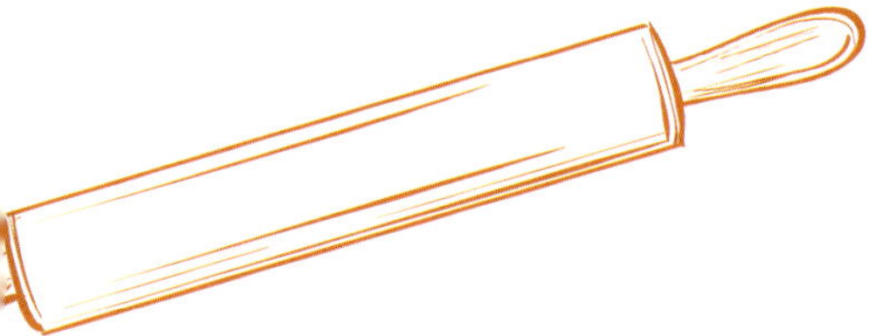

Faigy Murray

FOOD EDITOR, RECIPE DEVELOPER, AND PHOTOGRAPHER

I've been in the kitchen since I was a little girl. Over the years, my passion for all things cooking related led me to recipe developing and food blogging. I also launched my own spice line, Union Spice Blends, and published a cookbook, *My Pesach*. As a part of the Taste family, I love contributing recipes and sharing them with the Lakewood community. But the highlight of my week is sharing my editorials— little snippets of my life and food journey—with my readers.

Fun fact:

I wrote in a diary daily from when I was in second grade until I graduated seminary. That's probably why until today I love to write and express my feelings on paper.

Odaiah Leeds

RECIPE DEVELOPER

I'm a certified health coach, a graduate of the Institute for Integrative Nutrition, who is devoted to helping my clients develop happy and healthy lifestyles in a way that is flexible and individualized. I am passionate about creating nutritious, wholesome recipes that are packed with amazing flavor. I strongly believe that nobody should ever feel deprived while eating in a healthy way.

Nechama Norman

RECIPE DEVELOPER

I trained as a professional chef at the Jerusalem Culinary Institute, after which I wrote and developed recipes for an international magazine. I was also the original producer of Taste, where my recipes appeared monthly. My passion for helping people put my food career on the back burner; I now work full-time as a real estate agent in the New Jersey area, helping people sell and buy homes, though I still enjoy cooking and creating new recipes when I can squeeze the time in.

Chaya Ruchie Schwartz

RECIPE DEVELOPER AND PERSONAL CHEF

I'm the proprietor of CookIt, a home-cook business offering a meat and dairy menu. My specialty is the signature breakfast gifts that have been sent throughout Lakewood and beyond. I contribute recipes to Taste and prepare the recipes for the Taste photography shoots.

Fun fact:

As a teenager, I disliked the kitchen. My passion for cooking only started once I got married and hosted meals while living in Eretz Yisrael.

Tova Lowenthal

RECIPE DEVELOPER

I don't have a degree or fancy title before or after my name. So what am I? I am a Jewish mother just like you. In my spare time, I love playing around in the kitchen and trying new recipes to serve my family.

Atara Schechter

FOOD STYLIST

My first job with Taste was a Chanukah tablescape. What began as a passion for all things creative has turned into jobs with several publications. For me, tablescaping is an art: I see an empty table as a blank canvas where I get to create a composition that flows and encompasses our Jewish calendar. In addition to tablescapes and creative content, I enjoy doing food styling for Taste. It's fun to create a story with different foods using dishes, cutlery, textured napkins, flowers, and anything else I can think of.

Fun fact:

I like to serve individual portions when hosting guests. Everything is so much prettier and tastier when served in mini-portions.

Reuven Schwartz

RUBY STUDIOS,
FOOD PHOTOGRAPHER

Though I started out doing event photography, I eventually segued into the field of commercial photography with an emphasis on product photography. With precise attention to every aspect of the lighting and positioning, I love to get the perfect shot. I enjoy the creativity and the little details that go into photographing food.

Shaindy Siff

RECIPE DEVELOPER

I love to create new recipes, but my specialty and favorite thing to do is challenging myself to create delicious, creative recipes based solely on what I've got in my fridge and pantry. Because let's be real—creating meals quickly on demand is the real challenge!

Fun fact:

I may be a foodie who loves experimenting with tastes and flavors, but I won't touch any kind of fish no matter what.

Faigy Stein

RECIPE DEVELOPER

I've always loved baking and experimenting in the kitchen. My passion is creating recipes that are different, pretty, and delicious. In addition to my regular recipe columns in Taste, I also contribute recipes to various national magazines.

Fun fact:

My favorite baking tasks are fondant and frosting decorating.

Shaindel Steinberg

RECIPE DEVELOPER

I'm a recipe developer who loves to cook for the people around me. I create and cook easy, delicious recipes using basic ingredients, and I especially enjoy making healthy food without compromising on taste.

Fun fact:

I rarely measure when cooking. I cook something many times before calculating measurements for an exact recipe. This is why I avoid baking, which requires perfect measurements.

Bracha Waintman

RECIPE DEVELOPER

I specialize in creating delicious but healthful recipes that are quick and easy to make. My first recipes in Taste were those I developed while working as a personal chef. My other hobbies include teaching, playing music, and perfecting my photography skills.

Fun fact:

I rarely follow a recipe when I cook.

Esti Waldman

AKA ESTI PHOTOGRAPHY,
FOOD PHOTOGRAPHER

I originally started as a portrait photographer and gradually transitioned to food photography. Over the years, I've done work for several Jewish magazines, a couple of cookbooks, some major kosher brands and local businesses. Right now, most of my time is focused on Between Carpools. As one of the five women on the team, I contribute content and, of course, the photography.

Fun fact:

When I started my business as a portrait photographer, I left off my last name so that I could introduce myself around town and not be immediately identified as my business. It worked for a while, but then it just turned into another last name!

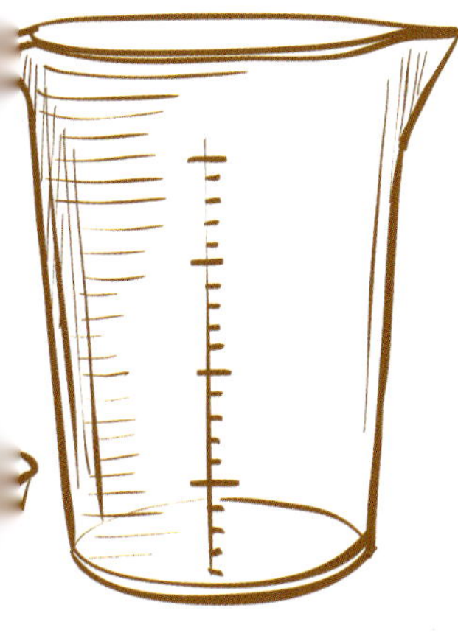

Ava Zuker

RECIPE DEVELOPER

I've always loved cooking and baking. As a child, I was constantly trying to learn more through watching my mother and grandmother, reading cookbooks, and watching cooking shows. I even started my own baking business, selling iced cookies and cake pops for *simchos*. I have also worked with Miriam Pascal at several food events and helped make a lot of the food in her cookbooks. When I was asked to join the Taste team, I was excited because sharing my own wholesome, easy, down-to-earth recipes was something I'd always wanted to do.

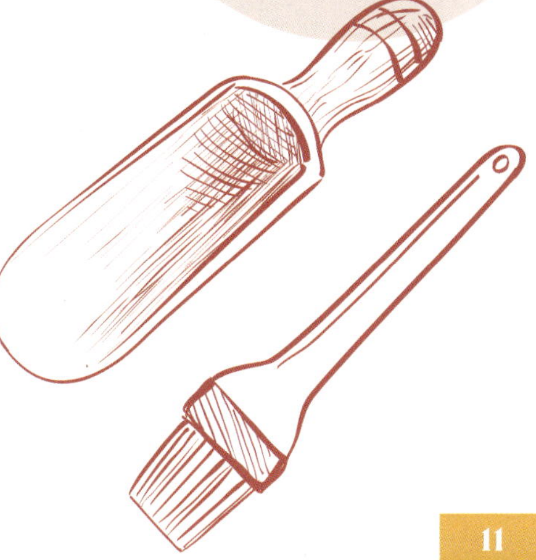

With thanks

Every acknowledgements page gives thanks first to Hakadosh Baruch Hu, and it is not—nor should it be viewed as—a trite thank-you. He was, is, and will always be the only constant, and without Him, none of this could ever be possible. *V'zacharta es Hashem Elokecha ki Hu hanosen lecha ko'ach la'asos chayil.*

Mr. Ari Berkowitz, publisher of *The Voice of Lakewood*, is the visionary behind the publication and all its affiliates. He gives us the ability to do more, reach higher, push for excellence. May Hashem bless all his efforts with success.

This is our first collaboration with Feldheim, and we are grateful for the expertise and professionalism of **Mr. Eli Hollander and the Feldheim team.** When we scouted reputable publishing houses for the publication of this cookbook, Feldheim was our first choice. Their *shem tov* in the Torah world and their *mentchlichkeit* in the professional sphere sealed the deal.

Nechama Norman was Taste's first food editor. In her capable hands the food magazine took shape; she carried it, named it, and gave it over to us. Nechama, we wish you much *hatzlachah* in all your endeavors, always!

Faigy Murray took over the reins as food editor in 2018 and has been at the job devotedly ever since. Faigy's mantra of good food that is easy and simple to prepare built on Taste's foundation. Thank you, Faigy, for your great taste!

Shevy Schottenstein served as Taste's managing editor and coordinator for years. With her expertise, attention to detail, and drive for perfection, she grew Taste into a food magazine par excellence. Thank you, Shevy!

Many thanks to **Shira Hoffman**, current coordinator and managing editor of Taste. With her can-do attitude, discerning eye, and exceptional copyediting skills, she makes her job seem easy when we know it's anything but. Shira, we're so glad you're part of the editorial team!

Thank you, **Adina Ribiat**, for bringing your extraordinary talent to Taste and *The Voice of Lakewood* each week. Over the many years we've been working together, your creativity has truly enhanced every aspect of the publication.

We knew *Taste's* cookbook layout would be in the right hands with the one and only **Perel Leah Levitin**. Thank you, Perel Leah, for listening to us and accommodating our requests and for the final, stunning product.

Chaya Ruchie Schwartz is not just another recipe contributor. Thank you, Chaya Ruchie, for preparing so many of these recipes for the photo shoots. In the food world, presentation is everything, and you've nailed it.

Thank you to all our **Taste contributors and photographers.** This cookbook is just a sampling of the hundreds of superb recipes and photos that Lakewood gets to revel in each week.

Finally, thanks to our broader Lakewood readership. We take pride in the knowledge that *The Voice of Lakewood* is truly your voice.

Aura Dweck and Malka Selengut

Editors, *The Voice of Lakewood*

starters & sides

Salmon and Roasted Veggie Skewers

The perfect appetizer—fresh and appealing.

Yield: 8 servings • pareve

SKEWERS

1 lb	boneless, skinless salmon, cubed
1	zucchini, cut into chunks
1	red pepper, cut into chunks
1	purple onion, cut into chunks
¼ cup	oil
1	frozen garlic cube
3 Tbsp	lemon juice
	Salt to taste
	Black pepper to taste

POPPY SEED DRESSING

¾ cup	oil
½ cup	sugar
¼ cup	vinegar
2 tsp	Dijon mustard
1 tsp	poppy seeds
Pinch	salt
Pinch	black pepper
1	box spring mix

1. **In** a large bowl, combine salmon, vegetables, oil, garlic, lemon juice, and spices. Toss to combine. Marinate for 10–20 minutes.

2. **Thread** veggies and salmon onto mini skewers. Grill or broil on medium-high for 7 minutes per side.

3. **In** a bowl, combine dressing ingredients.

4. **Assemble:** Place 2 mini skewers on a bed of spring mix and drizzle dressing on top.

5. **Serve** at room temperature.

Skewers can be refrigerated for up to 2 days.

Recipe by
Shaindy Siff

Styling and photography by
Chay Berger

starters & sides

Crispy Coated Cauliflower

The subtle sweetness and perfect crunch make this side a real winner.

Yield: 3–4 servings • pareve

2 Tbsp	oil
16 oz	frozen cauliflower florets, semi-defrosted
2	eggs, beaten
1 cup	honey-roasted peanuts
½ cup	bread crumbs
	Honey, for drizzling
	Oil spray

1. **Preheat** oven to 400°F. Pour the oil into a 9x13-inch pan.

2. **Place** cauliflower in a Ziploc bag. Add eggs and shake to coat.

3. **Crush** peanuts in a food processor fitted with the S-blade until they reach crumb consistency.

4. **Transfer** the peanuts to a second Ziploc bag, add the bread crumbs, and mix.

5. **Pour** cauliflower into crumb mixture and shake until well coated. Transfer to prepared pan.

6. **Drizzle** with honey, then spray with oil spray. Bake uncovered for 30 minutes.

Recipe by
Chaya Ruchie Schwartz

Styling and photography by
FP Photography

starters & sides

Garlic-Herb Sweet Potato Wedges

I'm always searching for hearty, delicious recipes that meet my whole family's approval. This side is great for a wholesome family dinner but nice enough to serve at a special get-together as well.

Yield: 5–7 servings • pareve

4	medium sweet potatoes
4	frozen garlic cubes
3 Tbsp	olive oil
1½ tsp	Italian seasoning
1 tsp	kosher salt
¼ tsp	black pepper

1. **Preheat** oven to 400°F.

2. **Cut** the ends off of the sweet potatoes. Scrub the skins and pat dry.

3. **In** a medium bowl, defrost garlic cubes. Add olive oil, Italian seasoning, salt, and pepper. Stir to combine.

4. **Cut** the sweet potatoes into wedges. Add to the bowl and toss to coat evenly.

5. **Lay** sweet potatoes in a single layer on a baking sheet.

6. **Roast** for about 45 minutes. For the last few minutes, broil on high to add extra crispiness.

Recipe by
Ava Zuker

Styling and photography by
FP Photography

starters & sides

Meat Egg Rolls

MEAT MIXTURE

1 lb	ground beef
2 Tbsp	ketchup
1 Tbsp	mustard
1	egg
⅛ cup	water
⅓ cup	cornflake crumbs
¼ tsp	salt
¼ tsp	garlic powder
¼ tsp	black pepper

SAUCE

2 cups	marinara sauce
3 Tbsp	apple cider vinegar
2 Tbsp	ketchup
1 Tbsp	brown sugar
20	egg roll wrappers, slightly defrosted

Yield: 20 egg rolls • meat

1. **In** a wide skillet, mix sauce ingredients and bring to a boil.

2. **In** a bowl, mix meat mixture ingredients.

3. **Place** a generous spoonful of meat onto an open egg roll wrapper, forming a line in the middle of the wrapper. Fold the short sides in and then roll it up, like a blintz. Seal edges with a drop of water. Repeat with remaining egg rolls.

4. **Cook** covered in the sauce in a single layer for 1¼ hours on low heat.

tip

This rewarms well.

Recipe by **Bracha Waintman**
Styling and photography by **Chay Berger**

Grilled Chicken Skewers

These skewers present beautifully! Reserve some marinade (before adding the chicken) to drizzle the plates before serving.

Yield: 4 servings • meat

¼ cup	honey
¼ cup	ketchup
3 Tbsp	brown sugar
2 Tbsp	soy sauce
1	frozen garlic cube
½ lb	chicken breast, cut into 1-inch cubes
1	red pepper, cut into 1-inch cubes
1	purple onion, cut into large chunks

1. **In** a bowl, combine honey, brown sugar, soy sauce, and garlic. Marinate chicken cubes in the sauce for 1 hour.

2. **While** chicken is marinating, soak skewers in water to prevent them from burning.

3. **Thread** chicken, pepper, and onion onto skewers and balance them over the sides of a foil pan so that the chicken is not touching the bottom of the pan.

4. **Bake** at 400°F for 22 minutes. For added flavor, baste chicken with leftover marinade halfway through baking.

Recipe by **Bracha Waintman**
Styling and photography by **Chay Berger**

Spiced Rice

This is a delicious spin on rice and 'roni. Kids and adults will love this textured side dish that's spiced just right.

Yield: 4 servings • meat/pareve

⅓ cup	olive oil
1 cup	white rice
1 cup	very fine noodles
2	onions, chopped
4	stalks celery, chopped
2	garlic cloves, minced
2 tsp	salt
1 tsp	dry mustard
1 tsp	dried cilantro
½ tsp	dried basil
½ tsp	dried ginger
¾ tsp	white pepper
½ tsp	onion powder
½ tsp	garlic powder
3 cups	chicken soup or pareve alternative

1. **In** a large pot, heat oil. Add rice, noodles, vegetables, and spices. Stir for 10 minutes.

2. **Add** chicken soup. Lower flame and cook for 10–15 minutes.

3. **Cover** and allow to sit for 10 minutes.

Recipe by
Nechama Norman

Styling and photography by
Esti Waldman

Korean Beef Kebabs

I actually got this recipe from my Korean manicurist, so you know it's the real deal. It has such amazing flavor! A must-have at your next barbecue.

Yield: 6 kebabs • meat

1½ Tbsp	red pepper paste
2	frozen garlic cubes
¼ cup	soy sauce
1 tsp	sesame oil
¼ cup	sugar
½ tsp	black pepper
2 lb	pepper steak or any thinly sliced meat

1. **In** a Ziploc bag, combine all ingredients except the meat. Add sliced meat and marinate in the refrigerator for 3 hours or overnight.

2. **Remove** meat from marinade and thread onto 6 skewers. Grill on medium-high for 6 minutes per side.

Recipe by
Shaindy Siff

Styling and photography by
Faigy Murray

starters & sides

Mini Garlic Hasselback Potatoes

These potatoes are different from the classic "salt, pepper, garlic powder" ones. The unusual blend of flavors sets them apart.

Yield: 3–4 servings • pareve

1 lb	baby red potatoes
8	frozen garlic cubes
1 Tbsp	coarse sea salt
1 tsp	black pepper
2 tsp	dry mustard
2 tsp	brown sugar
3 Tbsp	oil, for drizzling

1. **Preheat** oven to 400°F.

2. **Slice** the potatoes thinly, making sure to leave the bottoms intact.

3. **In** a small bowl, mix together garlic, salt, pepper, mustard, and brown sugar. Smear all over potatoes, making sure to get the rub in between the slices.

4. **Place** in a 9x13-inch pan. Drizzle oil over potatoes. Bake for 40 minutes.

Recipe by
Chaya Ruchie Schwartz

Styling and photography by
FP Photography

starters & sides

Ginger-Soy Green Beans

These green beans are perfect for a Shabbos side dish, and they heat up really well. Make a double batch because you won't be able to stop eating them; they're that addictive!

Yield: 4–6 servings • pareve

5 cups	fresh green beans
	Water
2 tsp	sesame oil
2 Tbsp	soy sauce
1 tsp	kosher salt
¼ tsp	ground ginger
1 tsp	garlic powder

1. **Place** green beans in a medium pot and fill with water to cover. Bring to a boil and cook for about 8–10 minutes or until desired tenderness is reached. Drain water.

2. **Add** the rest of the ingredients to the pot and toss to combine. Turn fire to medium and sauté for 3–5 minutes.

Recipe by
Ava Zuker

Styling and photography by
FP Photography

starters & sides

Pulled Beef

This never gets served without at least one request for the recipe—not to mention an empty tray. Serve over rice or mashed potatoes for a beautiful and delicious appetizer. Alternatively, serve with corn tortillas or taco shells, salsa, guacamole, and Tofutti sour cream for an easy and delicious dinner.

Yield: 6–8 servings • meat

3–4 lb	top-of-the-rib roast
1	red onion, diced
1 Tbsp	garlic powder
16-oz	bottle barbecue sauce
½ cup	ketchup
2 Tbsp	honey
	Water

1. **Preheat** oven to 300°F.

2. **Place** meat in a 9x13-inch pan. Sprinkle diced onion and garlic powder over meat. Add barbecue sauce, ketchup, and honey. Fill the barbecue sauce bottle with water and pour over everything.

3. **Cover** and bake for 4 hours.

4. **Pull** meat with 2 forks before serving.

Recipe by
Nechama Norman

Styling and photography by
FP Photography

starters & sides

Spinach-Pastrami Egg Rolls

When I made these the first time, I served them to a guest who doesn't like spinach, and he ate two whole egg rolls. When I told him what he was eating, he couldn't believe it— they were too good!

Yield: 12–14 egg rolls • meat

EGG ROLLS

	Creamed or sautéed spinach (see recipe below)
8 oz	turkey pastrami, diced
12–14	egg roll wrappers
	Oil for frying

EASY CREAMED SPINACH

1½ Tbsp	olive oil
1	small onion, minced
2	frozen garlic cubes
13-oz can	spinach, drained and squeezed dry
¼ tsp	salt
Dash	pepper
1	egg, beaten

1. **Prepare the spinach:** Sauté onion in oil until translucent, about 7 minutes. Add garlic and mix. Add spinach and stir until well combined. Turn off flame. Add salt and pepper. Allow to cool until mixture is warm but not hot.

2. **Add** egg and mix well.

3. **Turn** flame on low. Stir constantly until mixture thickens, about 5 minutes.

4. **Prepare the egg rolls:** Add pastrami to the creamed spinach and mix until combined.

5. **Place** 2 Tbsp spinach-pastrami mixture in each egg roll wrapper and fold up.

6. **Fry** on both sides until golden brown.

7. **Serve** plain or with duck sauce.

Recipe by
Nechama Norman

Styling and photography by
Esti Waldman

starters & sides

Asian Chicken-Stuffed Mushrooms

A modern appetizer with umami undertones. This is one appetizer that will please your guests.

Yield: 6–8 servings • meat

STUFFED MUSHROOMS

2 pints	cremini (baby bella) mushrooms
1 lb	ground chicken
⅓ cup	hoisin sauce
¼ cup	sliced scallions
	Sesame seeds, for garnish

HOISIN GLAZE

1 Tbsp	water
2 Tbsp	hoisin sauce

tip

You can cook this ahead of time and place under the broiler right before serving.

1. **Remove** stems from mushrooms, clean caps, and set aside.

2. **Preheat** oven to 400°F.

3. **In** a bowl, mix ground chicken with hoisin sauce and scallions (reserve a few tsp for garnish).

4. **Scoop** 1 Tbsp of the chicken mixture into each mushroom cap. Bake for 20 minutes or until chicken is cooked through.

5. **In** a bowl, mix glaze ingredients. Glaze the chicken, then place on the top rack in the oven and broil on low for 1–2 minutes, until slightly browned.

6. **Assemble:** Skewer mushrooms horizontally on medium-sized skewers and garnish with sesame seeds and reserved scallions.

Recipe by
Naomi Hazan

Styling and photography by
FP Photography

starters & sides

Roasted Rutabaga

This is a great, easy side dish for when you're having company and want to serve something different.

Yield: 8 servings • pareve

4 lb	frozen chopped rutabaga
⅓ cup	olive oil
1 Tbsp	salt
1 tsp	freshly ground black pepper

1. **Set** oven rack to the middle position and preheat oven to 450°F.

2. **Place** frozen rutabaga, oil, salt, and pepper in a large pan and mix thoroughly. Roast for 1½ hours, tossing every 30 minutes, until edges are blackened.

Recipe by
Dinah Bucholz

Styling and photography by
FP Photography

starters & sides

Skirt Steak Pinwheels

These are fairly simple to put together, great for entertaining, and delicious.

Yield: 6–8 skewers • meat

½ cup fresh pineapple, cubed

4 frozen garlic cubes

¼ cup teriyaki sauce

3 lb New York strip steak, cut into long, 1-inch-wide strips

1. **In** a bowl, combine pineapple, garlic, and teriyaki sauce.

2. **Place** meat in a bowl or Ziploc bag. Pour mixture over meat. Marinate in the refrigerator for at least 30 minutes, preferably overnight.

3. **Roll** pieces of steak into pinwheels and thread onto skewers (2–3 per skewer). Thread pineapple between the pinwheels.

4. **Place** over a 9x13-inch pan (the sticks should rest on the edges of the pan, with the meat suspended over it). Pour marinade over the meat, leaving excess liquid in the pan. Broil on high for about 4 minutes.

5. **Baste** meat with marinade from pan. Turn over and broil for another 3 minutes or until done.

Recipe by
Nechama Norman

Styling and photography by
Esti Waldman

soups

Butternut-Cauliflower Soup

This recipe is a family favorite. The flavor is just right, and the cauliflower gives the soup that perfect creamy texture.

Yield: 8 servings • pareve

2 Tbsp	oil
1	large onion, chopped
8 cups	vegetable broth
20-oz	bag frozen butternut squash
20-oz	bag frozen cauliflower
1 tsp	dried basil
	Salt to taste
	Black pepper to taste

1. **In** a large stockpot, heat oil and add onions. Sauté, stirring occasionally, until onions begin to brown and stick to the bottom of the pot.

2. **Add** a small amount of broth to deglaze the bottom of the pot. Add all remaining ingredients and bring to a boil. Reduce to a simmer and cook, covered, until all the vegetables are tender, 30–45 minutes.

3. **Purée** with an immersion blender.

4. **Serve** with toasted croutons.

Recipe by
Dinah Bucholz

Styling and photography by
FP Photography

soups

Dinner-in-a Bowl Soup

On a bone-chilling winter day, I called my sister for an idea for a "comfort soup." A little while later, the fragrant smell alone had warmed me up!

Yield: 12 servings • meat

2 Tbsp	oil
2 cups	finely diced carrots
7	frozen garlic cubes
1 cup	yellow split peas
1 cup	green split peas
½ cup	navy beans
½ cup	barley
2	thick chicken cutlets
14 cups	water
2 Tbsp	salt
	Black pepper to taste

1. **In** an 8-quart pot over medium flame, sauté carrots and garlic in oil until wilted and fragrant, stirring constantly for about 10 minutes. Add the rest of the ingredients and bring to a boil. Lower the flame and cook for 3 hours.

2. **Take** out cutlets and shred. Return to the pot and continue cooking for another 15 minutes.

3. **Serve** with baguettes for a complete supper.

Recipe by
Chaya Ruchie Schwartz

Styling and photography by
Chay Berger

soups

Celery Soup

I got this recipe from my sister's friend, who got it from her cousin, who got it from her friend… If everyone is making it, there must be a reason!

Yield: 15–18 servings • pareve

1 Tbsp	olive oil
2	onions, chopped
2	cloves garlic, chopped
2	bunches celery, sliced
2	small zucchini, sliced
12 cups	water
1 cup	oats
	Salt to taste
	Black pepper to taste

1. **In** a large soup pot over a medium flame, sauté onions and garlic in oil until translucent, about 8–10 minutes.

2. **Add** celery and zucchini and cook until soft, about 30 minutes. Add water and bring to a boil, then add the oats, salt, and pepper.

3. **Reduce** to a simmer and cook for 45 minutes.

4. **Using** an immersion blender, blend until smooth. Adjust seasonings to taste before serving.

Recipe by
Ava Zuker

Styling and photography by
FP Photography

soups

Chicken Sausage Gumbo

I've always had an affinity for Southern food; their dishes have such intense and vibrant flavors. When I had my family taste-test this recipe, the pot was licked clean—even my picky eaters enjoyed it!

Yield: 10 servings • meat

GUMBO

2 Tbsp plus ½ cup	oil, divided
2	large onions, diced
8	sausages (any flavor), sliced
2	green peppers, diced
3	boneless chicken breasts, cut into nuggets
1½ Tbsp	Creole seasoning (or see recipe below)
¾ cup	flour
8 cups	water

Creole seasoning is a traditional Southern spice mix that is used in a lot of Southern dishes.

CREOLE SEASONING

½ tsp	white pepper
½ tsp	black pepper
½ tsp	cumin
½ tsp	cayenne pepper
1 tsp	salt
½ tsp	chili powder
1 tsp	onion powder
1 tsp	garlic powder

1. **In** an 8-qt pot over a medium flame, sauté onions in 2 tablespoons oil until they begin to turn golden, about 10–15 minutes. Add sausages and sauté for 7–10 minutes. Add green peppers and sauté for 5 more minutes. Add chicken and sauté all together for 10–15 minutes. Add Creole seasoning and mix well.

2. **Meanwhile,** make a roux: In a small pot over a medium-high flame, heat ½ cup oil for 5 minutes. Add flour and whisk very well to make sure it doesn't clump. Lower the flame and continue stirring, watching it so it doesn't burn, until it is a light golden color.

3. **Add** roux to the pot of vegetables and meat and stir well.

4. **Add** water and bring to a simmer. Cook gumbo for about 1 hour, until thick.

Recipe, styling, and photography by
Faigy Murray

soups

French Onion-Pastrami Soup

This soup is so rich and filling, it's a hearty meal on its own.

Yield: 8 servings • meat

2 Tbsp oil

6 large onions, sliced

4 frozen garlic cubes

Salt

Black pepper

1–2 lb vacuum-packed pastrami

12 cups chicken broth

2 bay leaves

note

This recipe works well in a Crock-Pot: Place all ingredients in the Crock-Pot and cook on low for 5–10 hours.

1. **In** a large pot, sauté onions and garlic in oil with salt and pepper until onions are translucent.

2. **Add** pastrami, chicken broth, and bay leaves. Bring to a boil and allow to cook for 5 minutes. Lower the flame, cover the pot, and allow to simmer for 4–5 hours.

3. **Remove** pastrami, shred with 2 forks, and return to soup.

Recipe by
Shaindy Siff

Styling and photography by
Faigy Murray

soups

Tomato-Spinach Soup

Tomato and spinach are a natural pair. This soup tastes deceptively good; it really is healthful!

Yield: 6 servings • pareve/dairy

2 Tbsp	oil
1	large onion, chopped
2	garlic cloves, minced
4 cups	vegetable broth
28-oz	can diced tomatoes
2 cups	frozen chopped spinach
1 Tbsp	honey
	Salt to taste
	Black pepper to taste
1/4 cup	shredded cheese (optional)

1. **In** a large stockpot, heat oil and add onions. Sauté, stirring occasionally, until onions begin to brown.

2. **Add** garlic and mix until fragrant, about 30 seconds. Add a small amount of broth to deglaze the bottom of the pot.

3. **Add** remaining ingredients. Bring to a boil, then reduce to a simmer and cook covered for 20 minutes.

4. **Serve** with shredded cheese sprinkled on top and crusty bread on the side.

Recipe by
Dinah Bucholz

Styling and photography by
FP Photography

Broccoli-Asparagus Soup with Edamame Croutons

Not only does this soup taste great, it makes for a great presentation. The roasted edamame croutons are great for snacking on as well.

Yield: 12 servings • pareve

SOUP

1 Tbsp	olive oil
1	onion, chopped
3	garlic cloves, chopped
1	medium zucchini, chopped
24-oz	bag frozen broccoli florets
16-oz	bag frozen asparagus
8 cups	water
1 Tbsp	salt
½ tsp	black pepper
4	frozen basil cubes
4	frozen parsley cubes

EDAMAME CROUTONS

1½ cups	frozen shelled edamame
1 Tbsp	olive oil
½ tsp	garlic powder
¼ tsp	smoked paprika
½ tsp	kosher salt

1. **Prepare the soup:** In a large pot over a medium flame, heat olive oil. Add onion and garlic and sauté for about 10 minutes, until translucent.

2. **Add** zucchini, broccoli, and asparagus. Cook, stirring occasionally, for 45 minutes.

3. **Add** water, spices, and herbs. Cover, bring to a boil, and cook for 1½ hours.

4. **Blend** with an immersion blender.

5. **Prepare the croutons:** Preheat oven to 400°F. Line a baking sheet with foil.

6. **In** a medium bowl, mix all ingredients.

7. **Spread** out in a single layer on baking sheet. Roast for 30–40 minutes, stirring halfway through.

Recipe by
Ava Zuker

Styling and photography by
FP Photography

soups

Roasted Garlic Soup

If you love garlic like I do, this recipe is for you! Pair it with garlic bread and dinner is served.

Yield: 8 servings • pareve

3	whole garlic heads
1 Tbsp	oil plus more for drizzling
1	large white onion, sliced
¼ cup	white wine
2	large potatoes, diced
16 cups	water
2	beef stock cubes
	Salt
	Black pepper

1. **Preheat** oven to 400°F.

2. **Slice** off the top of each head of garlic so that the garlic is visible. Drizzle oil on top and wrap in foil. Bake for 30–40 minutes.

3. **In** a large pot, sauté onion in 1 Tbsp oil. Remove garlic from peel, add to the pot, and sauté for 5 minutes. Add wine and sauté for another 2 minutes. Add remaining ingredients.

4. **Bring** to a boil for 5 minutes, then lower flame and simmer for 1–2 hours.

5. **Using** an immersion blender, blend the soup until smooth.

Recipe by
Shaindy Siff

Styling and photography by
Faigy Murray

soups

salads

Beyond Quinoa Salad

This is my mother's specialty salad. You may be tempted to use canned corn instead of the real thing, but the taste doesn't compare!

Yield: 4 servings • pareve

SALAD

1 cup	quinoa
2 cups	water
1	sweet potato, thinly sliced into half rings
5 Tbsp	olive oil, divided
2	ears corn
1	zucchini, sliced into quarter rings
1	purple onion, chunked
12 oz	snow peas, chunked
8–10 oz	white mushrooms, sliced

DRESSING

	Juice of ¾ lemon (or 3/4 Tbsp lemon juice)
	Juice of ¼ lime (or 1½ tsp lime juice)
¼ cup	olive oil
	Salt
	Pepper

1. **Place** quinoa and water in a small pot and stir once. Bring to a boil, then lower flame and simmer for 20 minutes or until fully cooked. Cover pot and set aside.

2. **Preheat** oven to 450°F. Grease a 9x13-inch pan.

3. **Spread** sweet potato slices in the pan. Drizzle 2 Tbsp olive oil and roast until edges are brown and crispy, approximately 20 minutes.

4. **Peel** husk off the corn. Place corn in a pot of water and bring to a boil. Lower flame to medium-high and cook for 20 minutes. Using a sharp knife, slice chunks of corn off the cob. Set aside.

5. **Line** a baking sheet with parchment paper. Spread remaining vegetables on the baking sheet. Drizzle 3 Tbsp oil and roast for 30 minutes or until edges are brown and crispy. Gently toss vegetables and roast for an additional 20 minutes.

6. **Assemble:** In a large salad bowl, layer quinoa, sweet potato, grilled vegetables, and corn chunks. Squeeze lemon and lime over salad, sprinkle salt and pepper, and pour in the olive oil. Toss gently and serve warm.

Recipe by
Mirel Freylich

Styling and photography by
Chay Berger

Crunchy Cheese Salad

The smaller you dice the vegetables and cheese in this recipe, the crunchier your salad will be.

Yield: 6 servings • dairy

SALAD

4 oz	spring mix
4 oz	fresh mushrooms, minced
½	red onion, minced
3	sweet mini peppers, minced
6	slices pepper jack cheese, minced
1 cup	veggie sticks or terra sticks

DRESSING

3 Tbsp	vanilla Greek yogurt
½ cup	mayonnaise
2 Tbsp	lemon juice
1 tsp	mustard
1	clove garlic, minced
3 Tbsp	sugar
2	frozen parsley cubes
Dash	black pepper
2 Tbsp	water

1. **In** a large bowl, combine all salad ingredients.

2. **In** a small bowl, mix together dressing ingredients. Pour over salad right before serving.

Recipe by
Chaya Ruchie Schwartz

Styling and photography by
Faigy Murray

salads

London Broil Salad

This salad is a beautiful, classic appetizer.

Yield: 6 servings • meat

MEAT

1 cup	sweet red wine
¼ cup	honey
4	frozen garlic cubes
¾ lb	London broil
2	bay leaves

DRESSING

¾ cup	oil
½ cup	mayonnaise
3 Tbsp	sugar
1 tsp	lemon juice
1 tsp	garlic powder
1 tsp	mustard
1 tsp	soy sauce

SALAD

8 oz	romaine lettuce
1	large mango, peeled and cubed
1	cucumber, peeled and sliced into ½ rings
½ cup	candied pecans

1. **In** a small bowl, whisk together wine, honey, and garlic. Pour into a Ziploc bag and add London broil and bay leaves. Marinate in the refrigerator overnight.

2. **Place** meat in a 9x13-inch pan. Preheat broiler and broil meat for 10 minutes on each side. Allow to cool slightly and slice thinly across the grain, then slice larger pieces into thin strips.

3. **In** a medium bowl, combine dressing ingredients with an immersion blender.

4. **In** a large bowl, combine salad ingredients.

5. **Assemble:** On individual plates, form beds of lettuce. Place salad over lettuce. Place strips of meat over salad and drizzle dressing over everything.

Recipe by
Mirel Freylich

Styling by
Atara Schechter

Photography by
Ruby Studios

Ramen Salad

My favorite thing about this salad is the amazing crunch in every bite.

Yield: 8 servings • pareve

SALAD

3-oz	package ramen noodles
	Oil spray
4 oz	spring mix
2 cups	shredded purple cabbage
1 cup	shredded carrots
1	bunch scallions, sliced
1 cup	fresh mushrooms, sliced
½ cup	shelled, cooked edamame

DRESSING

1	ramen soup packet
¼ cup	oil
¼ cup	vinegar
3 Tbsp	sugar
¼ tsp	black pepper
1 tsp	black and white sesame seeds

1. **Preheat** oven to 350°F.

2. **Gently** crumble ramen noodles onto a baking sheet. Spray with oil spray and bake for 15 minutes, until golden.

3. **In** a large bowl, place all ingredients and toss to combine.

Recipe by
Shaindy Siff

Styling and photography by
Chay Berger

salads

Marinated Eggplant Salad

My sister-in-law used to make this for our family upon request. Eventually, she led me through the process of making it just right. This is the recipe with her perfect instructions.

Yield: 4 servings • pareve

½ cup	oil
1	medium eggplant, unpeeled, thinly sliced
⅓ cup	white vinegar
⅓ cup	water
⅓ cup	sugar
3	garlic cloves, crushed
½ tsp	salt

1. **In** a frying pan, heat oil and fry eggplant slices. Do not overcrowd pan. Fry on both sides until pieces are very dark and crispy (almost burnt).

2. **In** a bowl, whisk together white vinegar, water, sugar, garlic, and salt.

3. **Place** hot fried eggplant slices directly into marinade.

4. **Allow** to marinate overnight.

tip

I like to prepare a few eggplants at a time so that I have lots to put away. This usually doesn't come back into the kitchen once it goes out.

tip

This lasts in the fridge for 2 weeks.

Recipe by
Nechama Norman

Styling and photography by
Esti Waldman

salads

Mint-Infused Macerated Fruit Salad

Macerating is to fruit as marinating is to meat. Treat yourself to some big taste with this recipe. The mint gives it delicious bite, making it perfect for a long summer Shabbos afternoon.

Yield: 6 servings • pareve

2	peaches, diced
2 cups	grapes, halved
2 cups	fresh or frozen strawberries, halved
1 cup	fresh or frozen blueberries
2 Tbsp	orange juice
1 tsp	rum
1 Tbsp	fresh mint leaves, finely chopped

1. **Place** fruit in a bowl.

2. **In** a separate bowl, combine orange juice and rum. Pour over fruit. Mix in mint and allow to sit in the fridge for at least 30 minutes.

3. **Serve** with a dollop of fresh whipped cream or vanilla ice cream.

Recipe by
Nechama Norman

Styling and photography by
FP Photography

salads

Maple Salmon and Quinoa Medley

This is more than a salad—it's a meal in one. Take it to work for a filling lunch or serve it for supper; it's a winner either way.

Yield: 2–4 servings • pareve

SALAD

1 cup	quinoa
2 cups	water
1 tsp	salt
2	salmon fillets
¼ cup	teriyaki sauce
2 Tbsp	maple syrup
2 cups	purple cabbage
2	Persian cucumbers, cut into matchsticks
6	red mini peppers, cut into rings

DRESSING

3 Tbsp	olive oil
1 Tbsp	maple syrup
1 Tbsp	lemon juice
1 tsp	yellow mustard
1	frozen garlic cube
½ tsp	brown sugar
	Salt
	Pepper

1. **Preheat** oven to 350°F. Line a baking sheet with parchment paper.

2. **Place** quinoa in a small pot together with water and salt. Cook over high flame until it begins to boil, then allow to simmer until fully cooked, approximately 15 minutes. Strain with cold water and set aside.

3. **Cut** salmon into 1-inch cubes and place on baking sheet.

4. **In** a bowl, whisk teriyaki sauce and maple syrup together. Pour over salmon. Bake uncovered for 12 minutes.

5. **In** a small bowl, whisk dressing ingredients together.

6. **In** a wide, flat salad bowl, layer quinoa, purple cabbage, cucumbers, peppers, and salmon cubes. Drizzle dressing over salad and toss lightly.

Recipe by
Mirel Freylich

Styling and photography by
Chay Berger

Sweet Potato-Pomegranate Salad

This salad is super-refreshing, colorful, and crunchy. I always prepare a few sweet potatoes before Shabbos and serve this salad at all three meals, sometimes adding grilled chicken cutlets for the first course on Shabbos day.

Yield: 8 servings • pareve

SALAD

1	medium sweet potato, sliced into very thin circles
	Oil spray
8 oz	romaine lettuce
½ cup	pomegranate arils
½ cup	honey-glazed slivered almonds

DRESSING

½ cup	mayonnaise
½ cup	oil
3 Tbsp	sugar
1 Tbsp	vinegar
2	frozen garlic cubes
1 tsp	mustard
½ tsp	salt

1. **Grease** a baking sheet. Spread sweet potato on sheet and spray well with oil spray. Bake at 400°F for 30 minutes or until the ends start to brown and the middles are soft.

2. **In** a large bowl, combine lettuce, pomegranate arils, and sweet potatoes.

3. **In** a separate bowl, combine dressing ingredients. Blend with an immersion blender.

4. **Pour** dressing over salad and mix well. Garnish with almonds before serving.

Recipe by
Tova Lowenthal

Styling and photography by
Chana Rivky Klein

salads

Deli Salad with Fried Pretzel Crunch

With a little fried fun, this simple-to-prepare salad will be a great addition to your Shabbos-day seudah or anytime.

Yield: 4 servings • meat

SALAD

3 Tbsp	oil
¼ cup	pretzel nuggets
8 oz	lettuce
6	slices turkey deli, cubed
⅓ cup	cherry tomatoes, sliced
1	avocado, cubed

DRESSING

3 Tbsp	mayonnaise
4 tsp	water
1 tsp	mustard
1 tsp	garlic powder
1 tsp	sugar
½ tsp	salt
¼ tsp	pepper

1. **In** a small frying pan, heat oil. Fry pretzels for 3 minutes, flipping onto all sides. Drain and set aside.

2. **In** a small bowl, place all dressing ingredients and whisk until smooth.

3. **Assemble:** Layer lettuce, deli, cherry tomatoes, avocado, and pretzels in a salad bowl. Drizzle dressing over salad and toss prior to serving.

note

Although the pretzels taste best fresh, you can fry them up to 2 days in advance and store in an airtight container at room temperature.

Recipe by
Mirel Freylich

Styling and photography by
Chay Berger

salads

Salmon Sushi Salad

This phenomenal salad is sure to be a crowd-pleaser. It's perfect for any seudah, or you can serve it as a supper treat—it makes a great dinner in one.

Yield: 3 servings • pareve

RICE

1 cup	sushi rice
1¾ cups	water
3 Tbsp	rice vinegar
2 Tbsp	sugar
½ Tbsp	oil
½ tsp	salt

SALMON

2	salmon fillets
	Juice of ½ lemon
½ tsp	salt
¼ tsp	black pepper

SWEET POTATO

1	small sweet potato, peeled and cubed
2 Tbsp	oil
½ tsp	salt
½ tsp	black pepper

SPICY MAYO

3 Tbsp	mayonnaise
2 tsp	maple syrup
1½ tsp	sriracha sauce

2	Persian cucumbers, cut into matchsticks
1	avocado, diced
¼ cup	crispy fried onions

1. **Prepare the rice:** Rinse rice in a strainer for 2 minutes. Place in a pot with water, stir, and bring to a boil. Lower flame and allow to simmer for 15 minutes. Stir in remaining rice ingredients.

2. **Prepare the salmon:** Preheat the oven broiler. Grease a baking pan.

3. **Place** salmon in the pan. Sprinkle with lemon juice, salt, and pepper and broil for 10 minutes, uncovered.

4. **Prepare the sweet potato:** Preheat oven to 375°F. Line a baking sheet with parchment paper.

5. **In** a medium mixing bowl, toss sweet potato with oil, salt, and pepper. Spread onto baking sheet and bake for 15 minutes. Toss and bake for an additional 5 minutes.

6. **Prepare the spicy mayo:** In a small bowl, whisk together spicy mayo ingredients until smooth.

7. **Assemble:** In a large, shallow dish, form a bed of rice. Place remaining salad ingredients in strips across the top. Drizzle with spicy mayo.

Recipe, styling, and photography by
Mirel Freylich

salads

Broccoli Crumb Salad

Besides their great taste, cabbage salads are great for their long fridge life. Just make sure to pick out the nuts before storing.

Yield: 3 servings • pareve

SALAD

1	small sweet potato, peeled and cubed
2 Tbsp	oil
½ tsp	salt
½ tsp	black pepper
2 cups	purple cabbage
1 cup	riced broccoli
¼ cup	cashews
¼ cup	dried cranberries

DRESSING

2 Tbsp	oil
1 Tbsp	brown sugar
1 Tbsp	maple syrup
½ tsp	peanut butter
½ tsp	balsamic vinegar

1. **Preheat** oven to 375°F. Line a baking sheet with parchment paper.

2. **In** a medium mixing bowl, toss sweet potato with oil, salt, and pepper. Spread onto baking sheet and bake for 15 minutes. Toss and bake for an additional 5 minutes.

3. **In** a small bowl, whisk dressing ingredients together.

4. **Place** salad ingredients in a large salad bowl. Toss with dressing and serve.

Recipe, styling, and photography by
Mirel Freylich

salads

drinks & pops

Caramel Coffee Frappuccino

This refreshing drink is the perfect treat on a hot summer morning.

Yield: 1 serving • dairy

3 scoops	vanilla ice cream
1 cup	ice
1 cup	coffee, cooled
½ cup	milk
2 Tbsp	caramel syrup plus more for drizzling
	Whipped cream

1. **In** a blender, combine all ingredients except whipped cream. Blend until smooth.

2. **Pour** into a tall glass. Top with whipped cream and drizzle with caramel syrup.

Recipe by
Shaindy Siff

Styling and photography by
Chana Rivky Klein

Vanilla Chai Latte

The milky sweetness and warm spices will warm you up in seconds.

Yield: 1 serving • dairy

½ cup	water
2	chai tea bags
½ tsp	vanilla extract
1 Tbsp	maple syrup
¾ cup	milk
	Cinnamon

1. **Bring** water to a boil, then pour into a mug. Place 2 tea bags into the hot water and allow to steep for about 4 minutes. Squeeze remaining water out of tea bags, then discard.

2. **Add** vanilla extract and maple syrup to tea. Mix, then set aside.

3. **In** a small saucepan over medium-low heat, whisk milk until frothy. Pour milk into the mug of tea.

4. **Sprinkle** cinnamon on top.

Recipe by
Shaindy Siff

Styling and photography by
Chay Berger

drinks & pops

Chunky Brownie Fudgesicle

Your kids will thank you for making this indulgent and refreshing summer treat.

Yield: 5 pops • dairy

POPS

6 Tbsp	chocolate chips
1½ cups	low-fat plain Greek yogurt
3 Tbsp	milk
3 Tbsp	cocoa
1 tsp	vanilla extract
2 Tbsp	sugar
Pinch	salt
2 squares	brownies, chopped

TOPPINGS

	White and dark chocolate, for drizzling
2	sandwich cookies, crushed

1. **Melt** chocolate chips. Add the rest of the ingredients to the melted chocolate and mix until very smooth.

2. **Pour** into 5 ice pop molds. Freeze for 30 minutes, then add Popsicle sticks. Freeze overnight.

3. **Melt** white and dark chocolate.

4. **Once** frozen, place pops under running water to ease them out of the molds. Place on parchment paper.

5. **Working** quickly, drizzle melted chocolate over the pops and sprinkle with crushed cookies. Drizzle some more chocolate.

Recipe by
Chaya Ruchie Schwartz

Styling and photography by
Chay Berger

Reverse Hot Chocolate

There's something so comforting about a steaming mug of hot chocolate on a cold winter day. This is a twist on the classic hot cocoa.

Yield: 2 servings • dairy

HOT CHOCOLATE

2 cups whole milk (or 1 cup whole milk and 1 cup heavy cream)

½ tsp vanilla extract

¼ tsp cinnamon, optional

5 oz good-quality dairy white chocolate, chopped into small chunks

TOPPING

1 cup heavy cream

1 Tbsp confectioners' sugar

1 Tbsp unsweetened cocoa powder

1 oz white chocolate, grated, for garnish

1. **Prepare the topping:** In the bowl of an electric mixer, beat together cream, confectioners' sugar, and cocoa powder until soft peaks form.

2. **Prepare the hot chocolate:** In a saucepan, bring milk, vanilla, and cinnamon to a low simmer (do not boil). Add chopped white chocolate and stir constantly until melted.

3. **Pour** hot chocolate into mugs and top with a dollop of chocolate whipped cream and grated white chocolate.

Recipe by
Nechama Norman

Styling and photography by
FP Photography

drinks & pops

Blueberry Limonana

Stupendously refreshing, this drink will hit the spot in any setting.

Yield: 8–10 servings • pareve

1 cup	frozen blueberries, defrosted
5 cups	cold water, divided
1 cup	sugar
1 cup	boiling water
1 cup	fresh lemon juice (juice of 2–3 lemons)
	Mint leaves
	Ice cubes

1. **Place** blueberries and ¼ cup water in a blender and blend until smooth. Strain and discard pieces.

2. **Dissolve** sugar in boiling water and mix well. Pour into a large pitcher with a sealable lid. Add lemon juice, remaining cold water, blueberry puree, and mint leaves.

3. **Shake** well and serve with ice cubes.

Recipe, styling, and photography by
Mirel Freylich

drinks & pops

Delinut Coffee

If you thought you couldn't live without your morning coffee, try adding Delinut. It just gets better!

Yield: 2 servings • dairy

3 cups	brewed coffee
1½ cups	milk
½ cup	sugar
¼ cup	Delinut
	Marshmallows

1. **In** a saucepan over medium-low heat, combine all ingredients except marshmallows and stir until combined, approximately 5 minutes.

2. **Roast** marshmallows on stove flame until golden. Pour coffee into mugs and top with roasted marshmallows.

Recipe by
Shaindy Siff

Styling and photography by
Chay Berger

drinks & pops

Yogurt Pops

This is the perfect self-serve "ice cream treat" for when the kids come home from school or camp.

Yield: 12–15 pops • dairy

32-oz	container vanilla yogurt
½ cup	sugar
1 Tbsp	vanilla
3 Tbsp	sour cream
1 cup	granola
½ bag	frozen strawberries, slightly defrosted and diced

1. **In** a bowl, mix first 4 ingredients. Drop spoonfuls into 2-oz cups.

2. **Add** granola, then diced strawberries. Top with some more yogurt mixture.

3. **Add** lollipop sticks and freeze.

Recipe by
Chaya Ruchie Schwartz

Styling and photography by
Faigy Murray

Froyo Pops with Candy Chips

The healthy version of ice cream with some treats 'n' cheats!

Yield: 6 pops • dairy

1½ cups	frozen strawberries, defrosted
1	peach, peeled and chunked
5 oz	strawberry yogurt
¼ cup	milk
0.75-oz	raspberry-flavored fruit leather

1. **Place** all ingredients except fruit leather in a blender and blend until smooth.

2. **Add** fruit leather and pulse until chip-sized pieces form.

3. **Pour** into Popsicle molds and freeze until hardened, approximately 2 hours.

Recipe, styling, and photography by
Faigy Murray

Mint Hot Chocolate

Adding mint to hot chocolate is a delicious surprise!

Yield: 2 servings • dairy

1	quart milk
⅓ cup	unsweetened cocoa
½ cup	chocolate chips
1½ tsp	mint extract
	Whipped cream
	Red-and-white peppermint candies, crushed

1. **In** a large pot over medium-high flame, whisk milk and cocoa until fully combined.

2. **Add** chocolate chips and mint extract and whisk until melted and smooth.

3. **Pour** hot chocolate into glasses. Top with whipped cream and crushed candies.

Recipe by
Shaindy Siff

Styling and photography by
Chay Berger

drinks & pops

Mocha Caramel Ice Pops

For the coffee lover. (Aren't we all?)

Yield: 8 pops • dairy

3 Tbsp	coffee
½ cup	sugar
½ cup	hot water
1.75 oz	good-quality dark chocolate
½ cup	milk
	Caramel syrup for drizzling
	Chocolate syrup for drizzling
5.3-oz	container Greek vanilla yogurt

note

The freezing process might take a while, even overnight.

1. **Dissolve** coffee and sugar in hot water.

2. **In** a pot over low flame, mix chocolate and milk until smooth. Keep stirring to break up clumps.

3. **Shut** the flame and combine the two mixtures. Set aside to cool a little.

4. **Drizzle** the inside of Popsicle molds with caramel and chocolate syrup (or you can drizzle on the pops once frozen).

5. **Pour** mixture into molds, filling halfway. Drop spoonfuls of Greek yogurt into molds, then add coffee mixture until full.

6. **Freeze** for 30 minutes, then insert Popsicle sticks and continue freezing.

Recipe by
Chaya Ruchie Schwartz

Styling and photography by
Faigy Murray

drinks & pops

Fruity Smoothie

This is a delicious and refreshing drink, plus the color is gorgeous.

Yield: 4 servings • dairy

1 cup	frozen strawberries
1 cup	frozen blueberries
½ cup	frozen mango
½ cup	milk
1 cup	water
6-oz	container vanilla yogurt

In a blender, blend all ingredients together. Add water if too thick.

Recipe by
Gitty Friedman

Styling and photography by
Chay Berger

drinks & pops

Pumpkin-Spiced Latte

An autumn twist on a classic drink.

Yield: 6 servings • dairy

3 cups	whole milk
3 cups	strong brewed coffee
¼ cup	pumpkin puree
2 Tbsp	vanilla
⅓ cup	sugar
¼ tsp	cinnamon
2	cinnamon sticks
	Whipped cream, for garnish
	Ground cinnamon, for garnish

1. **In** a pot, combine milk and coffee and heat until almost boiling. Turn down flame.

2. **In** a small bowl, mix pumpkin puree, vanilla, sugar, and cinnamon until smooth. Add to pot and stir.

3. **Add** cinnamon sticks. Simmer over a low flame for about 30 minutes, being careful not to let it boil. Remove cinnamon sticks.

4. **Pour** into mugs. Top each mug with a dollop of whipped cream and a shake of cinnamon.

Recipe by
Nechama Norman

Styling and photography by
FP Photography

drinks & pops

Kiwi-Watermelon Pops

A great way to get your kids to eat "healthy"!

Yield: 12 pops • pareve

KIWI LAYER

3	kiwis, peeled and chunked
¼ cup	sugar
2 Tbsp	lemon juice
2 Tbsp	water

WATERMELON LAYER

3 cups	watermelon chunks
¼ cup	sugar

1. **Place** kiwi, sugar, lemon juice, and water in a blender and blend on high for 1 minute.

2. **Pour** into 12 Popsicle molds and freeze for 2 hours. Insert Popsicle sticks.

3. **Place** watermelon and sugar in a blender and blend on high for 1 minute.

4. **Pour** over kiwi layer and freeze for 2 hours.

Recipe, styling, and photography by
Mirel Freylich

drinks & pops

dairy

Vegetable Lasagna

I like to make this in advance and freeze it. Let it defrost on the counter, then pop it in the oven a half hour before serving.

Yield: 1 9x13-inch pan • dairy

1½ 26-oz   jars pizza sauce

1½   empty pizza sauce jars filled with milk

2   small zucchini, scrubbed and minced

8–10 oz   fresh mushrooms, cubed

1   box oven-ready lasagna

1 lb   shredded mozzarella cheese

tip

If you like your vegetables very soft, sauté them in oil before adding to the sauce mixture.

1. **Preheat** oven to 350°F.

2. **In** a bowl, mix sauce, milk, and vegetables.

3. **Pour** some sauce mixture into a 9x13-inch pan. Layer lasagna strips, sauce, and cheese. Continue until you have 3 layers.

4. **Bake** covered for 45 minutes. Uncover and bake for an additional 10 minutes.

5. **If** you'd like to freeze it, bake for 45 minutes, covered. To reheat, defrost, then add ¼ cup milk and ¼ cup shredded cheese to the top to keep it moist. Reheat for 20 minutes at 350°F.

Recipe by
Chaya Ruchie Schwartz

Styling and photography by
Chay Berger

dairy

Breakfast Banana Split

This gourmet breakfast dish has a little bit of everything in it. It's very filling, and the most amazing part? It's super-simple to prepare!

Yield: 4–6 servings • dairy

4	bananas
4 5.3-oz	containers vanilla Greek yogurts
	Blueberries
	Strawberries
	Granola (store bought, or see homemade granola recipe on page 116)
½ cup	peanut butter, melted

1. **Slice** bananas in half lengthwise. Pour yogurt in middle of the bananas. Top with fruit and granola.

2. **Drizzle** with melted peanut butter.

Recipe, styling, and photography by
Faigy Murray

dairy

Chocolate-Hazelnut Granola

This chocolate granola is one of my favorite homemade treats. Add it to plain yogurt, enjoy it in a bowl with milk, or snack on it straight out of the jar as is.

Yield: 3 cups • pareve

3 cups	rolled oats
1½ cups	coconut flakes
½ tsp	salt
¼ cup	brown sugar or coconut sugar
1 cup	hazelnuts, roughly chopped
⅓ cup	honey or maple syrup
⅓ cup	canola or coconut oil
1 tsp	vanilla extract
½ cup	cocoa powder

note

The dark color can make it difficult to tell when the granola is ready, so go by smell. Another way to tell is to taste the hazelnuts, since they take the longest to bake. They should taste pleasantly roasted and nutty.

1. **Preheat** oven to 350°F. Line a baking sheet with parchment paper.

2. **In** a large bowl, mix together oats, coconut flakes, salt, and sugar. Add chopped hazelnuts.

3. **In** a small bowl, whisk together honey or maple syrup, oil, vanilla, and cocoa powder. Pour over the oat mixture and toss until well coated.

4. **Spread** mixture on baking sheet and bake for 15–20 minutes. Remove from oven, stir, and bake for an additional 10 minutes.

5. **Store** in an airtight container or jar.

Recipe by
Sara Goldstein

Styling and photography by
Chay Berger

dairy

Cheesy Hash Browns

I believe that cheese on everything is always a good idea! This combination is delicious.

Yield: 4 servings • dairy

HASH BROWNS

4	potatoes, diced
1	pepper, diced
1	onion, diced
¼ cup	oil
½ tsp	garlic powder
½ tsp	salt
¼ tsp	black pepper

CHEESE SAUCE

1½ cups	shredded cheese blend
1 tsp	cornstarch
4	slices American cheese
⅓ cup	milk
1 tsp	mustard
Pinch	red pepper flakes
Dash	salt
Dash	black pepper

1. **Preheat** oven to 425°F. Line a baking sheet with parchment paper.

2. **In** a bowl, combine potatoes, pepper, onions, oil, and spices. Transfer to baking sheet.

3. **Bake** for 50 minutes, flipping twice during baking time.

4. **In** a bowl, mix shredded cheese with cornstarch.

5. **In** a small pot, combine cheese sauce ingredients and bring to a boil. Once the mixture has thickened, pour over hash browns.

tip

To shorten baking time, microwave the potatoes before baking.

Recipe by
Shaindy Siff

Styling and photography by
Faigy Murray

dairy

Ravioli in Pumpkin Alfredo Sauce

The combination of pasta and pumpkin spice is amazing.

Yield: 6 servings • dairy

26 oz	frozen cheese ravioli
½ cup	shredded cheese blend
1 tsp	cornstarch
1 cup	canned pumpkin puree
2 cups	heavy cream
⅛ tsp	nutmeg
	Fresh cracked black pepper

1. **Cook** ravioli according to package instructions.

2. **In** a bowl, combine shredded cheese and cornstarch.

3. **In** a pot, whisk pumpkin puree, cheese, heavy cream, and nutmeg. Bring to a boil.

4. **Pour** over ravioli. Sprinkle cracked black pepper over cheese.

Recipe by
Shaindy Siff

Styling and photography by
Chay Berger

dairy

French Toast Sticks

A new spin on an oldie-but-goodie recipe that's fun to make and fun to eat.

Yield: 10 sticks • dairy

1	medium challah
¾ cup	milk
2	eggs
1 Tbsp	oil plus more for frying
1 tsp	vanilla
½ cup	sugar
1 tsp	cinnamon

1. **Slice** challah into thick slices. Cut off the crust and slice into sticks.

2. **In** a bowl, whisk together milk, eggs, 1 Tbsp oil, and vanilla.

3. **Dip** the sticks into the mixture.

4. **Fry** in oil on both sides.

5. **Place** sugar and cinnamon in a bowl. Roll French toast sticks in sugar-cinnamon mixture.

Recipe by
Gitty Friedman

Styling and photography by
Chay Berger

Saucy Stovetop Frittata

If you don't like the pizza-saucy twist in this frittata, feel free to leave out the sauce and just add all of the cheese into the egg mixture before cooking.

Yield: 8 servings • dairy

1 Tbsp	oil
1	onion, diced
1	green pepper, diced
1	red pepper, diced
1	zucchini, diced
12	eggs
3 Tbsp	whole milk or heavy cream
1 cup	shredded mozzarella cheese, divided
½ tsp	salt
¼ tsp	black pepper
¼ tsp	garlic powder
1 cup	marinara sauce

1. **Preheat** oven to 425°F.

2. **In** a 12-inch cast iron skillet, sauté onion and peppers in oil until mostly soft. Add zucchini and sauté for 3 more minutes.

3. **In** a bowl, whisk eggs with milk, ½ cup cheese, salt, pepper, and garlic powder. Pour over vegetables. Cook on medium heat for 1–2 minutes, until edges begin to brown.

4. **Pour** marinara sauce over entire frittata and cover with remaining cheese.

5. **Transfer** skillet to the oven and bake for 10–12 minutes. Keep an eye on the frittata to make sure it doesn't burn.

6. **Serve** immediately.

Recipe by
Bracha Waintman

Styling and photography by
Chay Berger

dairy

Three-Cheese Ziti

Experience cheesiness like never before. A favorite for kids and adults alike!

Yield: 8 servings • dairy

1 lb	ziti, cooked and drained
1½ cups	shredded mozzarella cheese, divided
1½ cups	shredded cheddar cheese
1 cup	ricotta cheese
26-oz	jar marinara sauce

1. **Preheat** oven to 350°F.

2. **Place** pasta in a 9x13-inch baking dish. Add 1 cup mozzarella cheese, cheddar and ricotta cheeses, and marinara sauce and mix well. Sprinkle remaining mozzarella cheese on top.

3. **Bake** for 15 minutes or until crispy.

Recipe by
Shaindy Siff

Styling and photography by
Faigy Murray

Crepe Station

This is a fun activity in addition to a delicious breakfast. Each person can fill their crepe with their favorite flavors.

Yield: 8 crepes • dairy

CREPES

2	eggs
1 cup	milk
2 Tbsp	melted butter
1 cup	flour

OPTIONAL TOPPINGS

Strawberries and whipped cream

Marshmallow fluff and chocolate

Lotus cream and crushed lotus cookies

1. **In** a bowl, whisk together all crepe ingredients.

2. **Heat** a frying pan. Pour ⅔ cup of the mixture into the frying pan and tilt the pan until the batter covers the bottom. When the batter starts peeling away from the sides, flip the crepe over. Repeat for the rest of the batter.

3. **Top** with desired toppings.

Recipe by
Gitty Friedman

Styling and photography by
Chay Berger

dairy

Ricotta Tomato Tart

The creamy texture of this tart is so flavorful, you'll keep going back for more. Choose heirloom tomatoes in various colors for added appeal.

Yield: 8 servings • dairy

1	pie shell
2	Roma tomatoes
16-oz	container ricotta cheese
2	eggs
1¼ cups	mixed shredded cheeses, divided
¾ tsp	salt
⅛ tsp	black pepper
4	frozen garlic cubes
4	frozen basil cubes

1. **Preheat** oven to 450°F. Bake pie shell for 10 minutes.

2. **Slice** tomatoes into ¼-inch-thick slices and place on paper towels to drain liquid.

3. **In** a bowl, mix ricotta cheese, eggs, ¾ cup shredded cheese, salt, pepper, garlic, and basil until a smooth batter forms.

4. **Pour** cheese filling into tart and place tomatoes on top. Sprinkle ½ cup cheese on top.

5. **Bake** for 25 minutes, until cheese is golden.

Recipe by
Nechama Norman

Styling and photography by
Esti Waldman

dairy

fish

Seared Tuna with Tomato-Olive Relish

This recipe for fresh tuna makes the perfect light and delicious dish.

Yield: 4 servings • pareve

TUNA

2	tuna steaks
4 tsp	coarse sea salt
4 tsp	coarse black pepper
2 tsp	oil

RELISH

1 cup	Manzanilla olives, diced
½ cup	avocado, diced
½ pint	colored cherry tomatoes, diced
2 tsp	fresh parsley, chopped (or 1 tsp dried parsley)

1. **Rub** salt and pepper very well onto both sides of the tuna.

2. **Heat** oil in a frying pan until very hot. Add tuna. Cook for 60–120 seconds on 1 side and 30 seconds on the other.

3. **Prepare the relish:** In a bowl, combine olives, avocado, cherry tomatoes, and parsley.

4. **Serve** relish with the tuna.

tip

This relish is delicious with baked salmon as well.

note

My steaks were ½ inch thick. If yours are thicker, cook for 30 seconds longer. You want the white rim that you see in the picture, but you also want the inside to remain pink.

Recipe, styling, and photography by
Faigy Murray

fish

Broccoli and Salmon Wellington

If you're looking to impress, you'll want to make this! Use a whole side of salmon and make a big one, or prepare mini ones baked in muffin tins for perfect-sized appetizers.

Yield: 3–5 servings (or 6–8 appetizers) • pareve

1–2 Tbsp	oil
1	medium onion, diced
5 oz	fresh mushrooms, sliced
12 oz	frozen chopped broccoli
	Salt
	Black pepper
1 tsp	onion powder
1 tsp	garlic powder
1 sheet	puff pastry dough, thawed (or puff pastry squares, if making appetizers)
3 Tbsp	honey-Dijon dressing
1	large side of salmon, skinned (cut into 2-inch cubes for appetizers)
1	egg, beaten

variation

To make this as individual appetizers, preheat oven to 350°F and spray a muffin tin with oil spray. Spread approximately 2 tsp honey-Dijon dressing on each puff pastry dough square. Place 1 spoonful of the broccoli mixture on each. Add a salmon cube and sprinkle salt and pepper. Bring up the 4 corners and pinch to close. Place in muffin tin, brush with beaten egg, and bake until dough is golden.

1. **In a medium frying pan**, sauté onions and mushrooms in oil until translucent, about 15 minutes. Add frozen broccoli, 1 tsp salt, ¼ tsp pepper, and spices and cook until soft, about 10–15 minutes. Cool for a few minutes.

2. **Preheat** oven to 350°F. Line a baking sheet with parchment paper.

3. **Assemble:** Roll out puff pastry dough so that it's a little thinner and about 2–3 inches bigger. Spread honey-Dijon dressing over the middle third of the dough. Spread vegetable mixture in an even layer on top of the dressing.

4. **Place** salmon fillet on top of the vegetables. Sprinkle salt and pepper to taste.

5. **Cut** dough on either side into diagonal strips. Crisscross strips over salmon and tuck in ends. Brush with beaten egg.

6. **Place** on baking sheet and bake until golden and cooked through, about 30 minutes.

tip

Feel free to change it up and use other vegetables in place of the broccoli, such as spinach or a mix of sautéed onions, peppers, and zucchini. This recipe is also delicious with just sautéed onions and mushrooms.

Recipe by **Ava Zucker**
Styling and photography by **Faigy Murray**

fish

Fish Tacos

I love suppers that are easy, pretty, fun, and kid friendly. These tacos meet all of those criteria!

Yield: 6 servings • pareve

TILAPIA

6 slices	fresh tilapia
1 cup	flour
3	eggs, beaten
12 oz	flavored bread crumbs
	Oil for frying

COLESLAW

½ cup	mayonnaise
2	frozen garlic cubes
8 oz	shredded purple cabbage
6	corn tortillas

SPICY MAYO

1 cup	mayonnaise
1 Tbsp	sriracha sauce
1 Tbsp	lemon juice
1 tsp	chili powder

1. **Preheat** oven to 400°F.

2. **Prepare the tilapia:** Pat the fish dry. Dredge fish in flour, then dip into egg and then bread crumbs.

3. **Heat** the oil and fry on both sides for approximately 2 minutes or until golden.

4. **Prepare the coleslaw:** In a bowl, combine mayonnaise and garlic. Add cabbage and mix.

5. **Prepare the tortillas:** Toast corn tortillas on stovetop directly over the fire (flame should be the size of the tortillas) for about 5 seconds per side. Watch carefully—they burn in seconds!

6. **Prepare the spicy mayo:** In a bowl, mix ingredients until combined.

7. **Arrange** tortillas, fish, cabbage, and spicy mayo on the table, buffet style. Let your family have fun putting together their own tacos!

variation

You can bake the fish instead of frying it. Drizzle oil on a baking sheet and place the breaded fish on it. Bake for 20 minutes at 400°F, flipping halfway through.

Recipe, styling, and photography by
Faigy Murray

fish

Garlic-Butter Salmon

Serve this elegant dish on a Yom Tov or special occasion.

Yield: 8–10 servings • dairy

¼ cup	butter
15	garlic cloves, minced
1 bunch	parsley, minced, or 5 frozen parsley cubes
¼ cup	honey
2 tsp	salt
1 tsp	black pepper
	Juice of 1 lemon (approximately 2 Tbsp)
3 lb	salmon

1. **Preheat** oven to 400°F. Line a baking sheet with parchment paper.

2. **In** a small frying pan, melt butter. Add garlic. Cook until garlic is fragrant and beginning to brown. Add parsley and mix to incorporate. Add honey, salt, pepper, and lemon juice. Mix over a medium flame for about 3–5 minutes, until sauce thickens slightly.

3. **Lay** salmon on baking sheet and spread garlic sauce on top.

4. **Bake** for 20 minutes, then broil on high for 3 minutes.

5. **Best** served at room temperature.

Recipe by
Faigy Murray

Styling and photography by
FP Photography

fish

Flounder Roll-Ups

This recipe can be used with sole, flounder, or any other thin white fish. It works well with frozen fish fillets too—just make sure to defrost them fully before preparing.

Yield: 4 servings • pareve

¾ cup	tomato paste
3 Tbsp	mayonnaise
3 Tbsp	brown sugar
3 Tbsp	onion soup mix
1½ Tbsp	ketchup
⅓ cup	water
6	slices flounder

1. **In** a bowl, combine tomato paste, mayonnaise, brown sugar, onion soup mix, ketchup, and water.

2. **Spread** a thick layer on each fillet and then roll it up. (You may want to insert a toothpick to hold it together.) Place in a pan.

3. **Bake** uncovered at 350°F for 50 minutes.

Recipe by
Bracha Waintman

Styling and photography by
Chay Berger

fish

Moroccan Salmon

I am always amazed by the intense flavors that are features of some other cultures' cuisines. The flavors in this salmon just explode in your mouth.

Yield: 6 servings • pareve

6	slices salmon
3 Tbsp	oil
15-oz	can tomato sauce
2	medium ripe tomatoes, diced
4	garlic cloves
2	sprigs fresh cilantro or 4 frozen cilantro cubes
1 tsp	salt
1	jalapeño pepper, diced
1 tsp	cumin
1 tsp	paprika

1. **Preheat** oven to 350°F.

2. **Place** salmon in a 9x13-inch pan.

3. **In** a medium saucepan, heat oil and add the rest of the ingredients. Bring to a boil and let simmer for 30–35 minutes, checking on it occasionally.

4. **Pour** sauce over salmon. Cover and bake for 35 minutes.

tip

For a shortcut, simply buy good-quality matbucha, pour it over the salmon, and bake as instructed.

Recipe, styling, and photography by
Faigy Murray

fish

Stuffed Pesto Tilapia

The sauce in this recipe lends an amazing taste to the fish and potatoes, which become so soft that they literally melt in your mouth.

Yield: 7 roll-ups • pareve

2	medium potatoes, cooked and mashed
1 lb	tilapia fillets (1½ inches wide), pounded very thin
2 Tbsp	mayonnaise
1 Tbsp	oil
1 tsp	salt
2 Tbsp	teriyaki sauce
2	frozen basil cubes
2	frozen garlic cubes
½ tsp	mustard

1. **Place** approximately 2 Tbsp mashed potatoes in the center of each slice of tilapia. Roll up and place into a loaf pan, seam-side down. Line up the rolled tilapia slices very close together so they will keep their shape.

2. **In** a bowl, mix together mayonnaise, oil, salt, teriyaki sauce, basil, garlic, and mustard. Pour over tilapia.

3. **Bake** covered at 350°F for 40 minutes.

Recipe by
Tova Lowenthal

Styling and photography by
Chay Berger

fish

Something-for-Everyone Side of Salmon

This gorgeous and super-easy dish has gotten rave reviews every single time I served it. Displaying it on a bed of greens really completes the look.

Yield: 10 servings • pareve

3–4-lb	side of salmon
	Salt
	Black pepper
2 Tbsp	honey plus more for drizzling
2 tsp	Dijon mustard
¾ cup	crispy fried onions
½ cup	edamame, shelled and pulsed in the food processor until finely crushed
¼ cup	everything spice
¼ cup	sliced almonds
	Canola oil spray

1. **Line** a shallow 9x13-inch pan with parchment paper. Place salmon in the pan.

2. **Preheat** oven to 375°F.

3. **Sprinkle** salt and pepper over salmon. Smear honey and mustard on the salmon, making sure to coat the whole piece of fish.

4. **In** even sections, place fried onions, edamame, everything spice, and sliced almonds along the side of salmon. Spray generously with oil spray and drizzle some more honey.

5. **Bake** uncovered for 35–40 minutes.

6. **Serve** hot or at room temperature.

Recipe by
Chaya Ruchie Schwartz

Styling and photography by
Faigy Murray

fish

Salmon Lo Mein

This dish is a twist on a classic that is much easier to prepare. It also freezes beautifully.

Yield: 6 servings • pareve

1 large onion, thinly sliced

2 bell peppers, thinly sliced

2 carrots, thinly sliced or julienned

1 pint mushrooms, sliced

12-oz jar teriyaki sauce, divided

30 pieces cubed salmon

1 bunch scallions, sliced

1 box spaghetti, prepared according to package instructions

1. **Preheat** oven to 400°F. Line a baking sheet with parchment paper.

2. **In** a large bowl, combine all the vegetables except scallions with ¼ cup teriyaki sauce. Place on baking sheet in a single layer. Roast in oven for 15 minutes.

3. **In** a medium bowl, mix ¼ cup teriyaki sauce with salmon cubes.

4. **When** vegetables are ready, remove pan from oven and move vegetables to the side of the pan to create an empty section for the salmon. Place the salmon in a single layer in the middle of the veggies. Return pan to the oven for an additional 12 minutes.

5. **In** an extra-large bowl, mix remaining teriyaki sauce and sliced scallions with cooked spaghetti.

6. **When** salmon is ready, pour all the contents of the pan into the spaghetti bowl and toss carefully to combine.

Recipe by
Shaindel Steinberg

Styling and photography by
Faigy Murray

fish

Sea Bass with Fruit Salsa

Sea bass is a very pricey fish, so I like to reserve it for Yom Tov. It's so light, yet so flavorful.

Yield: 4 large servings or 6–8 small servings

FISH

- **4** slices sea bass
- Oil, for drizzling
- Salt
- Black pepper
- **2** garlic cloves, minced

SALSA

- **¼** purple onion, diced
- **1** large mango, diced
- **1** peach, diced
- **½** jalapeño pepper, diced
- Juice of 1 lime (about 2 Tbsp)
- **3** frozen cilantro cubes

1. **Preheat** oven to 400°F.

2. **Place** sea bass on a baking sheet and drizzle with oil. Sprinkle salt and pepper and rub garlic into fish.

3. **Bake** for 20 minutes. Cool and then refrigerate until ready to serve.

4. **In a bowl,** mix together salsa ingredients.

5. **Serve** salsa on top of the sea bass.

note

The salsa can be made 1–2 days in advance.

Recipe, styling, and photography by
Faigy Murray

fish

Lemon Pepper-Crusted Salmon

The secret to good salmon is to not overbake it. The general rule is 10 minutes per inch of fish, on a high temperature.

Yield: 4 servings • pareve

SALMON

4 1-inch-thick salmon fillets

Dried basil

Lemon pepper spice mix

Canola oil spray

TARTAR SAUCE

¼ cup mayonnaise

1 Tbsp pickle relish or ½ a dill pickle, finely diced

1 tsp sugar

1 tsp dried parsley

1. **Preheat** oven to 425°F. Line a baking sheet with parchment paper.

2. **Place** salmon on baking sheet. Generously coat with basil and lemon pepper, making sure to pat down the sides so that they are coated too. Spray with oil spray.

3. **Bake** for 10 minutes.

4. **For** a crustier top, cut baking time by 2 minutes and broil on high for an additional 4 minutes.

5. **In** a bowl, combine ingredients for the tartar sauce. Serve alongside salmon.

Recipe by
Bracha Waintman

Styling by
Atara Schechter

Photo by
Ruby Studios

fish

Fiery Batter-Dipped Fish Bites

Kid friendly and adult friendly—this one's a real keeper.

Yield: 4 servings • pareve

FISH

1¼ cups	flour
6 Tbsp	water
¼ cup	oil
2 Tbsp	sriracha sauce
2 Tbsp	sugar
1 tsp	salt
4	tilapia fillets, skinned
	Oil for frying

DIPPING SAUCE

5 Tbsp	mayonnaise
1 Tbsp	honey
2 tsp	mustard
	Black pepper to taste

1. **In** a medium-sized bowl, whisk together flour, water, oil, sriracha sauce, sugar, and salt.

2. **Cut** fillets into nuggets and stir into the batter until fully coated.

3. **In** a large skillet, heat ¼ inch oil. Fry fish for 2–3 minutes on each side, until golden brown. Drain excess oil.

4. **In** a small bowl, whisk together dipping sauce ingredients. Serve alongside fish.

chicken

Balsamic Roasted Chicken and Potatoes

All you need is 5 minutes for prep, and the result is a deliciously flavorful meal.

Yield: 4 servings • meat

CHICKEN

1 lb baby red potatoes, halved

1 onion, thinly sliced

4–6 chicken thighs

Salt to taste

Black pepper to taste

Mini peppers (optional)

Asparagus (optional)

SAUCE

½ cup balsamic vinegar

1½ Tbsp whole-grain mustard

2 Tbsp honey

3 frozen garlic cubes

Salt to taste

Black pepper to taste

1. **Preheat** oven to 400°F.

2. **In** a 9x13-inch baking dish, place potatoes and onion. Place chicken on top and season with salt and pepper.

3. **In** a bowl, combine sauce ingredients.

4. **Pour** sauce over chicken, making sure to get some under the skin.

5. **Bake** covered for 1 hour and 30 minutes. Baste chicken with sauce. Add mini peppers and/or asparagus if desired.

6. **Return** pan to oven and broil on high for about 5 minutes or until crispy.

Recipe by
Shaindy Siff

Styling and photography by
Chay Berger

chicken

Barbecue Skewered Cutlets

People are always on the lookout for good chicken cutlet recipes. Here is one of my favorites to add to your rotation.

Yield: 4 servings • meat

CHICKEN

½ cup	mayonnaise
¼ cup	barbecue sauce
1–2 cups	crushed barbecue corn chips
1 lb	chicken cutlets, cubed

DRESSING

⅓ cup	mayonnaise
1 Tbsp	honey
1 tsp	mustard
¼ tsp	soy sauce
1 Tbsp	water

Lettuce or spinach leaves

Sweet potatoes, cubed and roasted

1. **Preheat** oven to 375°F. Line a pan with parchment paper.

2. **Prepare the chicken:** In a small bowl, combine mayonnaise and barbecue sauce. Place crushed chips in a separate bowl. Dip chicken pieces into the mayo mixture and then into the chips.

3. **Thread** chicken onto skewers and "hang" over pan to catch the juices. Bake for 15–20 minutes, until cooked through, turning once halfway through.

4. **Prepare the dressing:** Place ingredients in a small bowl and whisk until combined.

5. **To** serve, place skewers on a bed of lettuce or spinach leaves with roasted sweet potatoes. Drizzle dressing over chicken.

Recipe by
Nechama Norman

Styling and photography by
FP Photography

chicken

Sesame Chicken Roll-Ups

A twist on the classic sesame chicken, yielding the same great taste plus an elegant presentation.

Yield: 12 roll-ups • meat

ROLL-UPS

½ cup	rice
1 cup	water
1 tsp	salt
½ cup	flour
1½ lb	chicken cutlets, pounded very thin

SAUCE

1½ cups	brown sugar
½ cup	ketchup
½ cup	duck sauce
3 Tbsp	oil
2 Tbsp	vinegar
1 Tbsp	mustard
2 Tbsp	sesame seeds

1. **Preheat** oven to 350°F.

2. **In** a pan, combine rice, water, and salt. Cover the pan tightly and bake for 1 hour.

3. **Remove** from oven and let rice cool a bit.

4. **Pour** flour onto a plate. Dip each chicken cutlet in flour so that the cutlets are thinly coated.

5. **Lay** cutlets on a flat surface. Place a handful of rice in the center of each cutlet and roll up. Place cutlets in a loaf pan, seam-side down, close together.

6. **In** a bowl, combine sauce ingredients. Mix well and pour over chicken.

7. **Cover** and bake for 30 minutes. Uncover and bake for an additional 15 minutes.

Recipe by
Tova Lowenthal

Styling and photography by
Chay Berger

chicken

Easy Chicken-Veggie Stir-Fry

So easy to make and so delicious... Don't count on any leftovers!

Yield: 4 servings • meat

STIR-FRY

2 Tbsp	oil
1	large onion, sliced
1	zucchini, chunked
1	red pepper, sliced into strips
1	yellow pepper, sliced into strips
1.5 lb	chicken breast
	Salt to taste
	Black pepper to taste

SAUCE

2	frozen garlic cubes
1 Tbsp	sesame oil
¼ cup	soy sauce
Dash	hot sauce
½ cup	duck sauce
2 Tbsp	flour
2 Tbsp	water

1. **In** a frying pan over medium flame, sauté vegetables in oil for 15–20 minutes, until slightly soft. Remove from pan and set aside.

2. **Cut** chicken into ½-inch-thick strips and lightly season with salt and pepper. Fry for 5–7 minutes per side.

3. **In** a bowl, whisk together sauce ingredients. Pour over chicken, stirring until mixture bubbles and thickens. Mix in veggies and cook on a low flame for 5 minutes.

4. **Serve** over rice or angel hair pasta.

Recipe by
Bracha Waintman

Styling and photography by
Chay Berger

Crispy Chicken Fingers

I've been making this salad dressing for years, and I always double it and store it in the fridge for whenever I need some. One day, I had cutlets defrosting and decided to experiment with the dressing. The results were amazing!

Yield: 4 servings • meat

CHICKEN

1.5 lb	chicken fingers
2 cups	Rice Krispies
½ tsp	chili powder

CREAMY HONEY-MUSTARD DRESSING

½ cup	mayonnaise
¼ cup	vinegar
1½ Tbsp	Dijon mustard
⅓ cup	honey
2	frozen garlic cubes
½ tsp	salt
¼ tsp	black pepper
½ tsp	onion powder
	Oil spray

note

You can use some of the remaining dressing on a salad.

1. **Preheat** oven to 375°F.

2. **In** a bowl, combine dressing ingredients and mix until smooth.

3. **Place** chicken fingers in a Ziploc bag with ½ cup of the dressing and marinate for 20 minutes.

4. **Place** Rice Krispies and chili powder in a bowl and mix to combine.

5. **Remove** chicken from Ziploc and discard the dressing. Dip chicken into Rice Krispies and press to adhere. Place in a pan and spray with oil spray.

6. **Bake** uncovered for 30 minutes.

Recipe by
Chaya Ruchie Schwartz

Styling and photography by
Faigy Murray

chicken

Curry Chicken

This recipe has a lot of ingredients, and I watched and measured as it was made two times to make sure I had it right. It was so worth the investment of time to learn how to make it properly. If you like a lot of flavor, this recipe is perfect for you.

SPICE MIXTURE

½ tsp	paprika
½ tsp	garlic powder
1 tsp	Lawry's seasoned salt
1 Tbsp	curry powder
½ tsp	white pepper

CHICKEN

8 pieces	chicken
½	medium onion, sliced
¼	green pepper, sliced
1 Tbsp	turmeric
¼ cup	oil
2	garlic cloves, sliced
¼ tsp	minced fresh ginger
½ cup	water
2	large carrots, cut into matchsticks
1	small potato, cut into matchsticks

Yield: 8 servings • meat

1. **Place** paprika, garlic powder, seasoned salt, curry powder, and white pepper in a large bowl or Ziploc bag. Add chicken pieces, onion, and pepper and toss to coat. Let sit for at least 30 minutes.

2. **In** a large skillet, combine turmeric, oil, garlic, and ginger. Stir over medium heat for 4–6 minutes, until oil becomes fragrant. Add chicken skin-side down together with onions and peppers and brown for about 6 minutes on each side.

3. **Add** water and continue cooking for 30 minutes. Add carrots and potatoes. Cover and cook for another 10 minutes.

4. **Serve** over rice.

Recipe by **Shaindel Steinberg**
Styling and photography by **Faigy Murray**

Mango Barbecue Drumsticks

This recipe happened by accident. It was dinnertime and I realized I was out of barbecue sauce, so I threw together a few ingredients that I had in the fridge...and a star was born.

Yield: 6 servings • meat

¼ cup	ketchup
1 Tbsp	honey
2	garlic cloves
1 Tbsp	soy sauce
1	mango, peeled and pitted (or 1 cup frozen mango cubes)
½ cup	barbecue sauce
12	chicken drumsticks

variation

Bake chicken in the oven, covered, at 400°F for 45 minutes. Then, either uncover and bake for another 20 minutes until crispy, brushing with reserved sauce a few minutes before done; or transfer to a grill, brush with reserved sauce, and grill on high for 2–3 minutes per side.

1. **Place** ketchup, honey, garlic, soy sauce, mango, and barbecue sauce in a blender and blend until smooth.

2. **Place** drumsticks in a large Ziploc bag and pour ¾ of the sauce over them. Seal bag and place in the refrigerator for at least 2 hours. Reserve remaining sauce in a container for later.

3. **Preheat** grill to 500°F. Lower flame to medium. Turn off 1 burner and place chicken skin-side down on the grill over the burner that is turned off. Close the lid of the grill and cook chicken for 10–15 minutes. Flip over and repeat on the other side for an additional 10–15 minutes, brushing with reserved sauce 2–3 minutes before done.

Recipe by **Shaindel Steinberg**
Styling and photography by **Faigy Murray**

Honey-Mustard Chicken Fingers

The juices in the marinade and the saltiness of the crumbs make this a deliciously moist and tasty dish. A great kid-friendly alternative to schnitzel!

Yield: 6 servings • meat

MARINADE

1½ cups	mayonnaise
¼ cup	honey
⅓ cup	mustard
2	garlic cloves
1 Tbsp	lemon juice
1–2 Tbsp	orange juice

CHICKEN

6	pieces chicken breast, cut into strips
2 cups	pretzel crumbs
	Oil spray

1. **In** a bowl, combine marinade ingredients.

2. **Dip** cutlets in marinade, then coat with pretzel crumbs.

3. **Place** in a single layer on a baking sheet and spray generously with oil spray. Refrigerate for at least 30 minutes.

4. **Preheat** oven to 400°F. Bake covered for 25 minutes. Uncover and bake for an additional 10 minutes.

Recipe by
Chaya Ruchie Schwartz

Styling and photography by
Faigy Murray

chicken

Hawaiian Chicken

It's sweet. It's tangy. It's delicious!

Yield: 4–6 servings • meat

¼ cup	light soy sauce
½ cup	pineapple juice
⅓ cup	brown sugar
2 Tbsp	ketchup
2	frozen garlic cubes
1	frozen ginger cube (optional)
1 Tbsp	sesame oil
2 lb	chicken breast, sliced thin

1. **Combine** all ingredients in a Ziploc bag.

2. **Massage** marinade into chicken. Marinate for 1 hour to overnight.

3. **Preheat** grill to medium-high heat. Grill chicken for 5–6 minutes on each side, basting chicken with remaining marinade as it's grilling.

Recipe by
Shaindy Siff

Styling and photography by
Faigy Murray

chicken

Pan-Fried Veggies and Nuggets

My sister-in-law gave me this delicious supper idea. Besides tasting great, it's really healthy since it contains no sugar.

Yield: 4 servings • meat

STIR-FRY

2 Tbsp	oil
1	onion, cut into chunks
1	small green pepper, cut into chunks
1	small red pepper, cut into chunks
2	garlic cloves
4	chicken cutlets, cut into 2-inch cubes
2 Tbsp	cornstarch

SAUCE

3 Tbsp	soy sauce
5 Tbsp	honey
6 Tbsp	water
2 tsp	rice vinegar
1 tsp	oil
1 tsp	cornstarch

1. **Sauté** onion, peppers, and garlic in oil for about 15 minutes.

2. **Meanwhile,** dredge cutlets in cornstarch.

3. **Once** vegetables are ready, take them out of the pan. Place cubed chicken in the pan and cook until just cooked through. Do not overcook. Set aside.

4. **In** the same pan, combine sauce ingredients except oil and cornstarch. Bring to a boil, then add oil and cornstarch and heat until thickened.

5. **Return** veggies and chicken to the pot. Cook for another 2 minutes.

Recipe by
Chaya Ruchie Schwartz

Styling and photography by
Faigy Murray

chicken

Shawarma Chicken Salad

Shawarma has always been a favorite of mine, but when bought at a takeout place and topped with everything they have to offer, the calorie count can be close to 1,000 (yes, for real!). I decided to create a lighter and healthier version with that intense flavor we all love.

Yield: 6–8 servings • meat

CHICKEN

- **1 Tbsp** oil
- **1** large onion, thinly sliced
- **2 lb** dark chicken cutlets or pargiyot, cut into bite-size pieces
- **3–4 Tbsp** shawarma spice

TOASTED PITA WEDGES

- **2** pitas, separated at the seams and cut into wedges
- Oil spray
- **1 tsp** salt
- **½ tsp** black pepper
- **2 tsp** garlic powder
- **1 tsp** onion powder
- **2 tsp** cumin

SALAD

- **8 oz** romaine lettuce, chopped
- **½ cup** diced tomatoes
- **½ cup** diced cucumbers
- **1 cup** diced Israeli pickles
- **4** Israeli hot peppers, chopped (optional)
- **¼ cup** prepared chickpeas
- Tahini dressing

1. **Prepare the chicken:** In a large frying pan, heat oil over medium-high heat. Add onion and sauté for about 5 minutes, until translucent. Add chicken and shawarma spice and mix until chicken and onion are coated evenly. Cook for 5 minutes, until chicken begins to brown. Cover and reduce flame to medium-low. Cook for 15–20 minutes, stirring occasionally, until chicken is cooked through.

2. **Prepare the toasted pita wedges:** Line a baking sheet with parchment paper and spray with oil spray. Lay pita wedges in pan in a single layer with the "insides" facing up and spray generously with oil spray. Sprinkle spices evenly over pitas. Bake at 375° for 10 minutes until crisp and golden around edges. Cool slightly before serving.

3. **Assemble:** Place lettuce in a large salad bowl. Top with vegetables and chicken and drizzle with tahini dressing. Serve with toasted pita wedges.

Recipe by
Shaindel Steinberg

Styling and photography by
Faigy Murray

chicken

Garlic-Herb Grilled Chicken

Let's be honest—grilled chicken can get boring. To make it more exciting, I try to come up with new recipes that add some variety. This chicken is super-easy, tasty, and light. It's good as is, sliced and put in a wrap, or cut up in a salad.

Yield: 3–4 servings • meat

3	frozen garlic cubes
2	frozen basil cubes
1	frozen dill cube
1	frozen parsley cube
1 Tbsp	olive oil
2	chicken breasts
	Oil spray

1. **In** a medium bowl, place garlic, basil, dill, parsley, and oil. Let the cubes defrost.

2. **While** cubes are defrosting, cut each chicken breast widthwise to create 2–3 thinner cutlets.

3. **Once** cubes are thawed, mix herbs and oil together. Add chicken cutlets and mix to coat evenly.

4. **Heat** a grill pan on medium-high heat. Spray with oil spray and grill chicken cutlets for about 4–6 minutes per side or until chicken is cooked through and has nice grill marks.

Recipe by **Ava Zuker**
Styling and photography by **FP Photography**

Lemon-Garlic Grilled Chicken

This is one recipe that I've had for ages. I cannot recall where I got it from, but thank you to whoever it was! It's simple and fresh and goes with everything.

Yield: 6 servings • meat

½ cup	olive oil
¼ cup	water
12	frozen garlic cubes or garlic cloves, crushed
1 tsp	salt
½ tsp	black pepper
2 lb	thin chicken cutlets or tenders
	Juice of 1 lemon
	High-heat cooking spray

1. **In** a large bowl, mix together oil, water, garlic, salt, and pepper. Add chicken. Cover tightly and marinate for 1 hour or overnight.

2. **Heat** grill to high.

3. **Add** lemon juice to the chicken. Mix well and let sit for another 10 minutes.

4. **Spray** grill with oil spray. Grill chicken for 2–3 minutes on each side, until inside is no longer pink.

Recipe by **Shaindel Steinberg**
Styling and photography by **Faigy Murray**

Light and Fresh Chicken Bottoms

I'm always on the lookout for good supper ideas. Here's a tried-and-true recipe shared by friends.

Yield: 6 servings • meat

2 Tbsp   honey
1 Tbsp   fresh lemon juice
½ tsp   cumin
1 tsp   garlic powder
¼ tsp   kosher salt
¼ tsp   black pepper
6   chicken bottoms

1. **Place** all ingredients except chicken in a large Ziploc bag and shake to mix. Add chicken and marinate in the refrigerator for about 2 hours.

2. **Preheat** oven to 350°F.

3. **Place** chicken in a pan and bake for 2 hours covered and 20 minutes uncovered.

Recipe by
Nechama Norman

Styling and photography by
Faigy Murray

chicken

Spicy Honey-Garlic Wings

Wings are a great entrée or main dish. Serve with a side of rice and steamed broccoli.

Yield: 4–6 servings • pareve

1.5 lb	chicken wings
2 Tbsp	sriracha sauce
¼ cup	honey
1 Tbsp	soy sauce
2 Tbsp	brown sugar, packed
1	garlic clove, minced
½ Tbsp	cornstarch
½ Tbsp	water
	Scallions, for garnish
	Sesame seeds, for garnish

1. **Place** chicken wings in a Crock-Pot.

2. **In** a bowl, whisk together sriracha sauce, honey, soy sauce, brown sugar, and garlic. Pour sauce over wings.

3. **Cook** on high for 1–2 hours or low for 3–4 hours.

4. **Line** a baking sheet with foil. When the wings are done, remove from Crock-Pot and place on baking sheet.

5. **Pour** the sauce into a medium-sized pot. In a bowl, whisk together cornstarch and water. Add to the pot. Cook over a high flame until thickened.

6. **Baste** the wings with the thickened sauce. Broil in the oven for 2–3 minutes.

7. **Garnish** with sesame seeds and scallions.

Recipe by
Sara Goldstein

Styling and photography by
Faigy Murray

chicken

Turkey Popper Baguettes

This recipe is not my usual style (bottled sauces, cooked turkey), but one day, I realized that the cutlets I had planned to make that night were not defrosted and supper had to happen fast. I opened my fridge and spotted a package of turkey breast, and the rest is history.

Yield: 2 servings • meat

3 Tbsp	oil
1	small onion, diced
8–12 oz	whole turkey breast, cubed
½ cup	barbecue sauce
¼ cup	duck sauce
2	baguettes
1	purple onion, sliced
	Romaine lettuce, shredded

1. **In** a saucepan over medium flame, sauté onion in oil until starting to brown. Add turkey and mix.

2. **Add** barbecue sauce and duck sauce and bring just to a boil.

3. **Serve** on baguettes with purple onion and romaine lettuce.

Recipe by
Nechama Norman

Styling and photography by
Faigy Murray

chicken

One-Pot Chicken and Rice

Chicken and rice is a staple in everyone's dinner plan. Making it this way is a great option because it only uses one pot, but also because you get an amazing crust from the rice—that's the part everyone can't get enough of!

Yield: 4 servings • meat

4	boneless chicken bottoms
½ tsp	kosher salt
⅓ tsp	black pepper
½ tsp	paprika
½ tsp	garlic powder
2 Tbsp	oil
1	onion, diced
3	frozen garlic cubes
1	carrot, diced
1	stalk celery, diced
1½ cups	rice
1½ Tbsp	chicken soup mix
3 cups	water

1. **In** a Ziploc bag, combine chicken and spices. Set aside to marinate for 10 minutes.

2. **In** a deep frying pan, heat oil and sauté onion, garlic, carrot, and celery for 3 minutes. Add chicken and sauté for 5 minutes on each side. Add rice, chicken soup mix, and water. Lower the flame, cover, and let simmer until the water has cooked out, about 25 minutes.

Recipe by
Shaindy Siff

Styling and photography by
Chay Berger

chicken

meat

Crock-Pot Chuck Roast

The quick prep makes this dish a perfect supper choice if you plan to be out all day.

Yield: 6 servings • meat

3 lb	chuck roast (in the net)
1 tsp	onion powder
1 tsp	paprika
½ tsp	salt
dash	black pepper
1 lb	colorful baby potatoes
2	sweet potatoes, chunked
3	stalks celery, sliced
1	onion, chunked
3	cloves garlic
⅔ cup	ketchup
2 cups	Coca-Cola

1. **Place** meat in Crock-Pot and sprinkle with spices. Add the rest of the ingredients and mix.

2. **Cook** on low for 6–8 hours.

Recipe by
Chaya Ruchie Schwartz

Styling and photography by
Chay Berger

meat

Eggplant-Meat Rollatini

In the past I wouldn't look at a recipe that required frying—until I came across this one. It's definitely worth the extra step, especially if you are a fan of eggplant, like I am.

Yield: 10 roll-ups • meat

¾ **lb**	chopped meat
4	eggs
⅓ cup	oats
1 tsp	salt
1 Tbsp	ketchup
1	large eggplant
2 cups	golden bread crumbs
	Oil for frying
2 cups	marinara sauce

1. **In** a bowl, combine meat, 2 eggs, oats, salt, and ketchup. Set aside.

2. **Peel** the eggplant and slice lengthwise into very thin slices.

3. **Prepare** 2 plates. In one, beat 2 eggs, and in the other, place the bread crumbs. Dip the eggplant slices into the eggs and then into the bread crumbs.

4. **In** a large frying pan over a medium-low flame, heat oil. Place 2 slices of eggplant at a time into the oil. Cook until eggplant starts to brown (about 3 minutes), then flip over. Cook on the second side until light brown. Remove from frying pan and repeat for remaining slices of eggplant.

5. **Place** approximately 2 Tbsp of the meat mixture into the center of each slice of eggplant. Roll up and place into a pan, seam-side down. Line up all the roll-ups close together in the pan. Pour marinara sauce over the eggplant.

6. **Bake** covered at 350°F for 1 hour.

Recipe by
Tova Lowenthal

Styling and photography by
Chay Berger

meat

Sweet Delmonico Roast

I often make this recipe when I have lots of guests. It's sweet and tangy and basically foolproof—and everyone always goes for seconds.

Yield: 8 servings • meat

1	onion, thinly sliced
3–4 lb	Delmonico roast
	Salt
	Black pepper
12-oz	jar Heinz chili sauce
12-oz	jar grape jelly
12-oz	bottle beer

1. **Preheat** oven to 350°F.

2. **Lay** sliced onion in a deep 9x13-inch pan. Place meat on top and sprinkle salt and pepper.

3. **In** a bowl, whisk chili sauce, grape jelly, and beer until smooth. The jelly can stay a bit chunky; it will melt while cooking. Pour sauce over meat.

4. **Bake** covered for 3–4 hours or until soft.

5. **Cool** completely before slicing. Return sliced meat to sauce.

Recipe by **Shaindy Siff**
Styling and photography by **Chay Berger**

Balsamic Red Wine French Roast

This may look like your typical roast, but the red wine and balsamic vinegar elevate it to a new level.

Yield: 8 servings • meat

3 lb	French roast or brick roast
2 Tbsp	oil, divided
2 tsp	salt
1 tsp	black pepper
2	large onions, thinly sliced
4	garlic cloves, crushed, or 4 frozen garlic cubes
¼ cup	balsamic vinegar
1 cup	red wine
½ cup	brown sugar

1. **Preheat** oven to 400°F.

2. **Rub** 1 Tbsp oil, salt, and pepper evenly into roast, massaging the spices in.

3. **Heat** a large frying pan. Brown the meat on all sides. Remove and place into a 9x13-inch pan.

4. **Add** 1 Tbsp oil and onions to the hot frying pan and sauté for 6–7 minutes, until beginning to brown. Add garlic and stir for 1–2 minutes, until fragrant. Add remaining ingredients, stir, and bring to a boil. Simmer for 15 minutes.

5. **Pour** over meat. Cover tightly and roast for 1 hour and 30 minutes.

6. **Allow** to cool. Slice meat and place back into juice. Cover and roast for another 1½ hours.

Recipe by **Shaindel Steinberg**
Styling and photography by **Faigy Murray**

Lamb Roast

The first time I ate lamb was at a family simcha. I was sold from the first bite!

Yield: 4–6 servings • meat

1 tsp	soy sauce
2 tsp	chicken soup mix
2 tsp	balsamic vinegar
	Salt
Dash	black pepper
1 tsp	paprika
2 tsp	crushed garlic
3 tsp	olive oil
2 lb	lamb roast

1. **In** a bowl, mix soy sauce, chicken soup mix, balsamic vinegar, spices, garlic, and oil together. Rub onto meat.

2. **Bake** at 200°F for 6–8 hours or overnight.

Recipe, styling, and photography by
Faigy Murray

Caramelized Onion Brisket

This recipe is so simple and has amazing results. Super-soft and flavorful!

Yield: 8 servings • meat

3	large white onions, thinly sliced
⅓ cup	sugar
2 Tbsp	oil
5 lb	second-cut brisket
	Salt
	Black pepper
7-oz	bottle beer

tip

To freeze: Freeze whole. Defrost, slice, return to the sauce, and reheat covered at 350°F for 1 hour.

1. **Preheat** oven to 350°F.

2. **In** a bowl, combine onions, sugar, and oil and set aside.

3. **Sprinkle** salt and pepper on each side of the brisket. Rub to make sure brisket is evenly coated.

4. **Place** brisket in a pan and pour beer on top. Place onion mixture on the brisket. Gently pat the onions so they stick to the meat.

5. **Bake** covered for 3–4 hours, until soft.

6. **Once** cooked, refrigerate before slicing, then return meat to the sauce.

Recipe by **Shaindy Siff**
Styling and photography by **Chay Berger**

Breaded Veal Chops

Veal chops are just as easy to prepare as schnitzel, but their price tag marks them for special occasions.

Yield: 6 servings • meat

6	veal chops
½ cup	flour
4	large eggs, beaten
2 cups	seasoned bread crumbs
	Oil for frying

1. **Dredge** chops in flour. Dip in beaten eggs, then in bread crumbs.

2. **In** a large frying pan, heat oil. Fry the chops in batches over medium-high heat until golden brown, 3–5 minutes per side. Drain on paper towels.

Recipe by
Dinah Bucholz

Styling and photography by
FP Photography

meat

Oven-Baked Pepper Steak

This is adapted from my mother's staple pepper steak recipe, which calls for sautéing and cooking in a pot. I simplified it so it's baked in just one pan in the oven—way easier and just as delicious!

Yield: 4 servings • meat

2 lb	pepper steak
1	onion, diced
1	red pepper, cut into thin strips
4-oz	can mushrooms
2 Tbsp	soy sauce
2 Tbsp	onion soup mix
1½ cups	water
1 tsp	sugar
½ tsp	garlic powder
¼ tsp	black pepper

1. **Preheat** oven to 350°F.

2. **Place** meat and vegetables in a 9x13-inch pan.

3. **In** a bowl, mix the rest of the ingredients together. Pour over meat and veggies. Cover pan tightly and bake for 2 hours.

4. **Serve** over rice.

Recipe by
Chaya Ruchie Schwartz

Styling and photography by
Faigy Murray

meat

One-Pan Beef Bolognese

Growing up, this was my favorite dinner. It's super-easy and delicious.

Yield: 4 servings • meat

2 Tbsp	oil
1	onion, diced
3	garlic cloves, chopped
1–2 lb	ground beef
1 tsp	kosher salt
½ tsp	black pepper
1 tsp	garlic powder
28-oz	can crushed tomatoes
	Water
1 lb	pasta

1. **In** a large pot, heat oil. Add onion and garlic and sauté for approximately 3 minutes. Add beef and spices and sauté until browned. Add crushed tomatoes. Fill the empty can with water 1½ times and add to the pot.

2. **Bring** to a boil and pour in pasta. Lower the flame, cover the pot, and allow to simmer until water has cooked out, approximately 20 minutes.

Recipe by
Shaindy Siff

Styling and photography by
Chay Berger

The Heart of Our Home

Yitti Berkovic

My daughter wants to bake.

It is two hours to Shabbos, my kitchen is immaculate, and my daughter wants to bake.

She wants to take out the mixer, powder my countertops with flour, slick grease into measuring cups, and splash batter onto oven doors.

She wants to puff clouds of cocoa, leave stubborn streaks of melted chocolate on the refrigerator handles, and drip yolk into grooves in the cabinets I didn't know were there.

Help!

I love her dearly. I appreciate that she wants to, uh, pitch in. And she says she'll clean up *everything*, and she really means it, with all the sincerity an 11-year-old girl can muster.

But a mother (occasionally) knows best,

and a mother has the almost prophetic ability to see into the future. I know what will happen when clean-up time hits: dear daughter of mine will suddenly have a million and one things she *has to* do; she'll need to straighten her hair for Shabbos or search through her closet to find a missing Shabbos shell, and I'm going to be the one left holding the *shmatte* and the Windex bottle.

So, I want to say no.

I want to say, "*Mammale*, thank you so much for your offer, but I have a store-bought *kokosh* cake sitting proudly on the counter, a counter that has been scrubbed and scoured and now gleams. I don't need you to bake anything this week. Maybe a different time."

Out of habit (maybe it's a survival instinct?), I start shaking my head, and my daughter's face falls.

"You always tell me 'now is not a good time.' If now isn't a good time, when will there ever be a good time?"

Now *my* face falls.

I don't want to admit it, not to her and not to myself, but she's right.

I remember when I first toured my current home, back when I saw my kitchen for the first time. My husband and I trailed hopefully behind the oh-so-perky realtor, trying to imagine how a house filled with some other family's furniture, and some other family's memories, would someday feel like home.

Though the house had its charms (and its flaws), I found myself drawn to the kitchen. Its floor plan was open and inviting, and the island in its center was spacious, with plenty of room for little elbows and helping hands.

I knew then that I wanted my kitchen to be the heart of my house, the place where my family gathered, noshed on cookies, schmoozed about their day, rolled up their sleeves to peel potatoes and dice onions, and kvetched that their siblings weren't helping enough ("I peeled six potatoes and he only peeled three!").

I wanted my kitchen to be joyful and busy and to smell delicious. I wanted my cookbooks to be splattered and stained, battered, and bruised, telling stories of the guests who came for Yom Tov, new mothers who enjoyed their delivered suppers, and, yes, kids who experimented in the kitchen, baking cakes that got stuck in their Bundt pans but still tasted scrumptious.

(I also wanted my kitchen to magically clean itself, but the realtor refused to accommodate.)

Baruch Hashem, after a few handshakes and wire transfers, the house became ours, and just as I had hoped, the kitchen became the place where I spend most of my time. Maybe it isn't as Norman Rockwell-like as I imagined; sure, I cook and bake, host and schmooze, and serve up hot meals and cold meals here in my kitchen—but I also use this spot to clean and clean and clean. Some weeks I worry that I spend more time in here with Mr. Clean than I do with the human denizens of my home.

So, I don't want to clean again—not even to accommodate my daughter's budding baking skills. But then I remember that daughters learn a lot from their mothers in the kitchen, not only about how we make our food, but about *why* we make our food.

Food can be inspiring, not only in its artistry but also in its generosity.

I may not be the most natural in the kitchen. My doughs don't always bounce, my vegetables don't always caramelize, and my whips aren't always stiff. Maybe my daughter (if she's ever allowed to practice) will have finer culinary skills than I have, but she can still learn other, equally important cooking skills from me.

She can learn that the reason the kitchen is the heart of our home is because the work we do here is our family's lifeblood. We cook when we are tired, and we cook when it is inconvenient. We stand on our feet early in the morning and well into the night, we chop when our eyes are only half open, and we put up supper even when we know our kids are going to ask for instant soup. And then, when

we wash the pots, scrub the counters, and mop the floors, we know those ingredients are invaluable too; they are ingredients that help our children feel healthy, secure, and loved.

We know, even when we are bone-tired, when we don't want to cook or clean ever again, that our efforts are a small price to pay for a reward so great: the way our loved ones' eyes light up when the flavor hits their palate—sweet, sour, bitter, tangy, tart. More than that, it's the joy they have knowing we worked long and hard for them because we love them, because we want them to feel cared for, because we thought about them more than we thought about ourselves.

So, even though it's two hours to Shabbos and my kitchen is immaculate, I give my daughter the green light.

Go ahead, sweetie. Roll up your sleeves.

Make your mess (and feel free to introduce yourself to Mr. Clean), and savor the sweetness of stretching yourself to give to others.

It already smells delicious. I can't wait to have a taste.

desserts

Cake Kabobs

We all love a pretty dessert that requires little effort to put together. The prep time for these kabobs can be cut down by buying store-bought brownies and cubed fruit. Have fun with any variation you can think of!

Yield: 6 servings • pareve

BROWNIES

1 stick	margarine
½ cup	cocoa
2	eggs
Pinch	salt
¼ cup	flour
1 cup	sugar
1 tsp	vanilla
1 cup	chopped walnuts (optional)

FUDGE SAUCE

⅓ cup	cocoa
¾ cup	sugar
5 oz	whip topping
½ stick	margarine

KABOB OPTIONS

Pineapple

Strawberries

Mango

Kiwi

Marshmallows

Caramel syrup

1. **Preheat** oven to 350°F. Grease an 8x8-inch pan.

2. **Prepare the brownies:** In a pot, melt margarine and cocoa. Mix until smooth. Shut the flame.

3. **Add** 1 egg at a time and mix quickly. Add the rest of the ingredients and mix well. Pour into the pan.

4. **Bake** for 45–50 minutes. The center may be a bit raw; it will continue baking while it's still hot.

5. **Prepare the sauce:** In a pot, bring cocoa, sugar, whip topping, and margarine to a boil.

6. **Assemble:** It's best to assemble the kabobs when the cake is cold or frozen. Cut cake into cubes and string the cake, fruit, and marshmallows onto skewers.

7. **Drizzle** caramel syrup and serve with fudge dipping sauce.

.... *note*

The sauce can be made in advance and reheated.

Recipe by
Chaya Ruchie Schwartz

Styling and photography by
Chay Berger

desserts

Berry Blend Galette

This stunning and delicious dessert can be prepared in minutes with no mixer in sight. It's my go-to dessert when I'm having company.

Yield: 6 servings • pareve

DOUGH

1½ cups	flour
1 Tbsp	sugar
¼ tsp	salt
1 stick plus **1 Tbsp**	margarine, chilled
4 Tbsp	water

FILLING

2½ cups	fresh or frozen berries (I used strawberries, blueberries, and cherries)
¼ cup	sugar
2 Tbsp	cornstarch
1 Tbsp	flour (only if using frozen fruit)
½ tsp	cinnamon
2 Tbsp	raspberry or apricot jam, divided
	Sugar, for sprinkling

1. **In** a bowl, mix dough ingredients by hand until a smooth dough forms. Flatten into a disc and refrigerate in a Ziploc bag for 1 hour.

2. **Preheat** oven to 350°F.

3. **In** a bowl, combine filling ingredients.

4. **Once** chilled, roll out dough between 2 pieces of parchment paper to form a 12-inch circle.

5. **Smear** 1 Tbsp jam in the center of the dough. Place a heaping mound of the filling in the center, leaving a 2-inch border. Fold the dough over the edge of the fruit, pleating as you go around. Brush with remaining jam and sprinkle some more sugar.

6. **Bake** for 30 minutes.

7. **Serve** at room temperature.

Recipe by
Chaya Ruchie Schwartz

Styling and photography by
Chay Berger

S'mores Popcorn

This delicious treat is easier to make than the typical s'mores but packs the same punch, and since it includes lite popcorn, we can call it "healthy."

Yield: 6 servings • pareve

4 oz	dark chocolate
1 cup	boiling water
5 cups	lite popcorn
5	graham crackers, chopped but not crushed
1 cup	mini marshmallows

note

If you are preparing this for a later time, allow to cool completely before storing.

1. **Preheat** oven to 375°F.

2. **Place** chocolate in a Ziploc bag. Place bag with chocolate into boiling water and let it sit for 10–15 minutes.

3. **Line** a baking sheet with parchment paper. Pour popcorn onto baking sheet and spread out evenly. Sprinkle graham crackers and marshmallows over popcorn.

4. **Remove** bag of chocolate from water and dry the outside of the bag well. Snip a tiny corner off the bag and drizzle chocolate all over the ingredients on the baking sheet. Bake for 5 minutes.

Recipe by
Shaindel Steinberg

Styling and photography by
Faigy Murray

desserts

Dream Ice Cream in a Jar

My classic ice cream recipe—all dressed up for any occasion!

Yield: 15 small Mason jars • pareve

CHOCOLATE CRUMBS

- **1½ cups** flour
- **1½ cups** sugar
- **5 Tbsp** cocoa
- **1½ tsp** baking powder
- **1 tsp** baking soda
- **¾ cup** oil
- **½ cup** light brown sugar

CHOCOLATE ICE CREAM

- **16 oz** whip topping
- **8 oz** coffee creamer
- **3.5-oz** package chocolate pudding

VANILLA ICE CREAM

- **16 oz** whip topping
- **8 oz** coffee creamer
- **3.5-oz** package vanilla pudding

1. **Preheat** oven to 350°F. Line a baking sheet with parchment paper.

2. **Prepare the crumbs:** In a bowl, combine all crumb ingredients and mix well. Pour onto baking sheet and bake for 15 minutes. Allow to cool. Crumble once cooled.

3. **Prepare the ice cream:** In the bowl of an electric mixer, beat whip until stiff. Add coffee creamer and chocolate pudding and mix.

4. **Repeat** for vanilla ice cream.

5. **Assemble:** Place 1 Tbsp crumbs into Mason jars. Fill a pastry bag with vanilla ice cream and fill the jars halfway. Add another Tbsp of crumbs. Freeze until firm. Fill a pastry bag with chocolate ice cream and fill until almost the top. Add another Tbsp of crumbs. Freeze.

Recipe by
Faigy Stein

Styling and photography by
Chay Berger

desserts

Stuffed Apple Bake

Bring simple baked apples to a whole new level.

Yield: 6 servings • pareve

6	Red Delicious apples
2	Cortland apples
2 tsp	sugar
½ tsp	cinnamon
⅓ cup	chopped walnuts
2 Tbsp	brown sugar
1 Tbsp	margarine

1. **Preheat** oven to 350°F. Line a baking sheet with parchment paper.

2. **Using** a sharp knife, cut out the top half of each Red Delicious apple's core.

3. **Peel**, core, and grate remaining apples.

4. **In** a small bowl, mix grated apples with sugar and cinnamon.

5. **Stuff** apple holes with shredded apple mixture.

6. **In** a small bowl, combine nuts, brown sugar, and margarine. Using a fork, mash the margarine into the nuts and sugar until a crumbly mixture forms. Press over the shredded apple mixture.

7. **Wrap** each apple in foil and place on baking sheet. Bake upright for 40 minutes. Open the foil slightly and bake for 5 more minutes.

Recipe by
Mirel Freylich

Styling and photography by
Chay Berger

Chocolate Bits-and-Nut Caramels

The nuts and chocolate give these caramels extra crunch, taking them to the next level. You will need a candy thermometer for this recipe.

Yield: 4 dozen • dairy

2 cups	roasted and salted mixed nuts
1 cup	chocolate chips
1 cup	unsalted butter
2 cups	brown sugar, packed
1 cup	light corn syrup
¼ cup	water
14 oz	condensed milk (sweetened milk cream)
1 tsp	vanilla extract

1. **Grease** a 9x13-inch pan. Place a large piece of parchment paper (bigger than the pan) into the pan. Pour the nuts and chocolate chips into the pan.

2. **In** a large pot, melt butter. Add brown sugar, corn syrup, and water and bring to a boil. When boiling, add the condensed milk. Stir constantly until an inserted candy thermometer reaches 248°F. Remove from heat, add extract, and stir.

3. **Pour** mixture over the nuts and chocolate. Let sit for 10 minutes before transferring to the refrigerator. Chill until hard.

4. **Lift** caramel out of the pan and cut. If caramel is too hard to cut, let it sit out a little to soften. Wrap each caramel individually in wax paper or a waxed candy wrapper.

Recipe by
Chaya Ruchie Schwartz

Styling and photography by
Faigy Murray

desserts

Reese's Puffs Ice Cream Pie

A peanut butter lover's dream come true.

Yield: 2 pies • pareve

56-oz	container pareve vanilla ice cream, defrosted
2½ cups	Reese's Puffs cereal, divided
1 tsp	vanilla extract
2	graham cracker pie crusts
½ cup	peanut butter
½ cup	baking chocolate

1. **In** a food processor, place ice cream, 2 cups Reese's Puffs, and vanilla extract and blend until smooth. Pour into pie crusts.

2. **In** a microwave-safe bowl, melt peanut butter and chocolate together. Drizzle over ice cream pie. Sprinkle remaining Reese's Puffs on top.

3. **Freeze** for at least 2 hours before serving.

Recipe by
Shaindy Siff

Styling and photography by
Faigy Murray

desserts

Éclair in a Jar

This éclair in a jar is just creamy and dreamy. If you use the shortcuts, it's super-simple to throw together, too.

Yield: 10–12 small Mason jars • pareve

CRUMBS

2	sleeves graham crackers

CUSTARD

4 cups	pareve milk
1 tsp	margarine
1 Tbsp	vanilla sugar
4	eggs
½ cup	sugar
3 Tbsp	cornstarch

CHOCOLATE GANACHE

8 oz	baking chocolate
½ cup	whip topping

1. **Prepare the crumbs:** In a food processor, process graham crackers until fine crumbs form.

2. **Prepare the custard:** In a pot over medium flame, cook pareve milk, margarine, and vanilla sugar until simmering, stirring constantly. Remove mixture from heat before it comes to a boil.

3. **In** a bowl, whisk eggs, sugar, and cornstarch until sugar is dissolved.

4. **Return** the pot to heat. Slowly, stirring constantly, add egg mixture and cook until custard is thick enough to coat the back of a spoon (approximately 5–10 minutes).

5. **Allow** to cool at room temperature or refrigerate until ready to use.

6. **Prepare the ganache:** Chop the chocolate into small pieces and place in a bowl.

7. **In** a pot over medium flame, heat the whip topping until almost boiling.

8. **Pour** heated whip topping over prepared chocolate. Mix well with a fork until a shiny and smooth chocolate ganache forms.

9. **Allow** to cool and thicken at room temperature before piping.

10. **Assemble:** Place 1 spoonful crumbs in each Mason jar. Fill a pastry bag with custard and pipe over the crumbs. Spoon on another layer of crumbs. Pipe another layer of custard. Top with crumbs. Fill a Ziploc bag with chocolate cream, snip off an edge, and pipe on top.

variation

Short on time? You can replace the homemade custard with 2 containers store-bought custard and the homemade ganache with 1 container store-bought chocolate cream. (If you prefer a less intense custard flavor, you can whip up 1 16-oz container whip topping and combine it with 1 container custard.)

Recipe by
Faigy Stein

Styling and photography by
Chay Berger

Layered Fruity Ice Cream

A beautiful, refreshing dessert for Shabbos or Yom Tov.

Yield: 1 9x13-inch pan • pareve

ICE CREAM BASE

4	eggs, separated
8 oz	whip topping
½ cup	sugar

SAUCE

2 cups	frozen strawberries, defrosted
2 cups	frozen mango, defrosted
½ cup	orange juice, divided
½ cup	sugar, divided

1. **Prepare the ice cream:** In the bowl of an electric mixer, beat egg whites until stiff.

2. **In** a separate bowl, beat whip topping until stiff. Add in egg yolks and sugar.

3. **Carefully** fold whip mixture into the egg whites. Divide into 2 bowls.

4. **Prepare the sauce:** In a food processor or blender, blend strawberries with ¼ cup orange juice and ¼ cup sugar.

5. **Separately,** blend mango with ¼ cup orange juice and ¼ cup sugar.

6. **Carefully** fold the strawberry sauce into one bowl of ice cream, reserving a bit of sauce for drizzling. Repeat for the mango ice cream.

7. **Spread** the strawberry ice cream in the bottom of a 9x13-inch pan. Carefully spread mango ice cream on top. Freeze for at least 12 hours.

8. **Drizzle** with remaining sauces before serving.

Recipe by
Bracha Waintman

Styling and photography by
Chay Berger

desserts

Deconstructed Peach Crumble

I love the combo of something warm and fruity with creamy, cold ice cream. This recipe can be made on a busy day and serves beautifully.

Yield: 6–8 servings • pareve

FRUIT MIXTURE

2	large fresh peaches, peeled and sliced
3 Tbsp	brown sugar
1½ tsp	oil
½ tsp	cinnamon
	Juice of ½ lemon

CRUMBS

¼ cup	oil
¾ cup	old-fashioned oats
⅓ cup	brown sugar
¼ cup	flour
½ tsp	cinnamon

Pareve vanilla ice cream

Caramel syrup

1. **Prepare the fruit mixture:** Preheat oven to 350°F.

2. **In** a bowl, combine all ingredients, coating fruit well. Place in a pan.

3. **Cover** and bake, stirring periodically, for about 1 hour or until fruit is soft and juice has thickened. Uncover and bake for an additional 10 minutes.

4. **Prepare the crumbs:** Combine ingredients and place in a pan. Bake for 20 minutes, until golden brown. Allow to cool and store in a container.

5. **Assemble:** Spoon warm fruit mixture into glass dishes. Add a scoop of vanilla ice cream to each dish. Sprinkle crumb topping over ice cream. Drizzle caramel syrup.

Recipe by
Nechama Norman

Styling and photography by
Esti Waldman

Fruit Salsa and Cinnamon Chips

This recipe is so refreshing! The combination of flavors is a feast for the palate. The salsa is best served fresh.

Yield: 4 servings • pareve

FRUIT SALSA

1	pink grapefruit, peeled
1 cup	watermelon
1 cup	fresh pitted cherries
1 cup	strawberries
2 tsp	lemon juice
3 Tbsp	raspberry preserves

CINNAMON CRISPS

4	6-inch wraps
2 tsp	cinnamon
2 Tbsp	sugar
	Oil spray

1. **Prepare the salsa:** Dice fruit as small as possible. Add lemon juice. Add the preserves up to 1 hour before serving.

2. **Prepare the crisps:** Preheat oven to 400°F. Cut each wrap into 6 triangles and lay in a single layer on a baking sheet. Sprinkle generously with cinnamon and sugar and spray with oil spray. Bake uncovered for 10 minutes or until crispy.

3. **Serve** chips alongside the fruit salsa.

Recipe by
Chaya Ruchie Schwartz

Styling and photography by
Faigy Murray

desserts

Creamy Confection In a Jar

A beautiful, delicious trifle, with the option of using store-bought ingredients. Just don't show anyone the ingredient list if you took the shortcuts...

Yield: 7 Mason jars • pareve

CHOCOLATE-COFFEE CREAM

1 cup	whip topping
2 Tbsp	coffee
8 oz	baking chocolate
8 oz	white baking chocolate

CARAMEL

1 cup	light brown sugar
8 Tbsp	margarine
½ cup	whip topping
2 Tbsp	corn syrup
1 Tbsp	vanilla sugar

NUT CRUNCH TOPPING

2 cups	coconut flakes

1. **Prepare the cream:** In a pot, heat whip topping until almost bubbling. Shut the flame and add coffee, mixing until dissolved.

2. **Place** chocolate in a bowl. Pour coffee mixture over chocolate and allow to sit for 3 minutes before mixing well. Allow to cool before layering.

3. **Prepare the caramel:** In a pan over low heat, combine brown sugar, margarine, whip topping, and corn syrup. Stir frequently until margarine is melted.

4. **Increase** heat and bring to a boil.

5. **Boil** for exactly 2 minutes and then remove from heat. Allow to cool for 5 minutes.

6. **Add** vanilla sugar and stir well. Allow to cool before layering.

7. **Prepare the topping:** Preheat oven to 325°F.

8. **Spread** flakes on a baking sheet in a thick layer. Bake for 5–10 minutes, until golden. Allow to cool before using.

9. **Assemble:** Place chocolate-coffee cream in a large pastry bag, or place in a Ziploc bag and cut a hole in the corner. Pipe cream into Mason jars, filling them approximately ⅓ of the way.

10. **Place** caramel cream in a large pastry bag, or place in a Ziploc bag and cut a hole in the corner. Pipe on top of chocolate-coffee cream, filling approximately another ⅓ of the way.

11. **Top** with nut crunch.

Use 1 container store-bought pareve chocolate cream, adding 1 tsp instant coffee granules dissolved in 1 tsp boiling water to cream and mixing to combine; 1 container store-bought pareve caramel cream; and 1 container store-bought nut crunch.

Recipe by
Faigy Stein

Styling and photography by
Chay Berger

desserts

Cookiedillas

This jumbo cookie "quesadilla" is so simple to put together and so fun to eat! Serve on a platter and let your family dig in.

Yield: 2 9-inch cookiedillas • pareve

COOKIES

1½ sticks	margarine
1 cup	brown sugar
1 cup	white sugar
¾ tsp	vanilla extract
2	eggs
2 cups	flour
1 tsp	baking soda
Pinch	salt
¾ bag	chocolate chips

FILL-INS

8 Tbsp	chocolate hazelnut spread
	Fresh strawberries, cleaned and sliced
	Caramel syrup
	Sea salt, for sprinkling

1. **Preheat** oven to 350°F. Grease 4 9-inch round pans.

2. **Cream** margarine with sugars, then add the rest of the ingredients until well combined. Divide dough evenly among the 4 pans.

3. **Bake** for 35 minutes or until golden.

4. **Once** cooled, flip over 1 cookie pie onto a platter and smear 4 Tbsp chocolate hazelnut spread on it. Add sliced strawberries, drizzle caramel syrup, and sprinkle some sea salt.

5. **Top** with the second cookie.

6. **Repeat** with the other 2 cookie pies.

note

Do not use frozen fruit. You can replace fresh strawberries with mango, pineapple, or any fruit of your choice.

Recipe by
Chaya Ruchie Schwartz

Styling and photography by
Chay Berger

desserts

baked goods

Amaretto Cake with Apple-Spiced Streusel

For a twist on an all-time favorite classic, I paired the cake with a delicious apple-spiced streusel.

Yield: 1 Bundt pan • pareve

CAKE

2 cups	flour
2 cups	sugar
2 tsp	baking powder
⅔ cup	oil
4	eggs
1 package	instant vanilla pudding
¾ cup	orange juice
¼ cup	amaretto liqueur
¼ cup	vodka

STREUSEL

1 cup	flour
½ cup	brown sugar
½ cup	sugar
1 stick	margarine
½ tsp	cinnamon
¼ tsp	nutmeg
⅛ tsp	allspice
Dash	ginger

ICING

1½ cups	confectioners' sugar
1 tsp	vodka
1 tsp	amaretto liqueur
1 Tbsp	orange juice

1. **Preheat** oven to 350°F. Grease a Bundt pan.

2. **Using** a hand mixer, mix all cake ingredients until just combined.

3. **In** a separate bowl, mix streusel ingredients by hand until crumbly.

4. **Pour** batter into Bundt pan, then cover the batter with crumbs, pressing some of the crumbs into the batter.

5. **Bake** for 45 minutes.

6. **Once** cooled, combine icing ingredients and drizzle over cake.

Recipe by
Chaya Ruchie Schwartz

Styling and photography by
Chay Berger

Nutty Biscotti

These biscotti are great for munching on when you're craving something sweet.

Yield: 24 biscotti • pareve

1 cup	oil
2	eggs
1 cup	sugar
1 cup	brown sugar
2 tsp	vanilla extract
3 cups	flour
1 tsp	salt
1 tsp	baking soda
1 cup	chopped walnuts
⅓ cup	dried cranberries
½ cup	chocolate chips

1. **Preheat** oven to 350°F. Line a baking sheet with parchment paper.

2. **In** a large bowl, mix oil, eggs, sugar, brown sugar, and vanilla extract until fully combined. Add flour, salt, and baking soda and continue to mix. Fold in nuts, dried cranberries, and chocolate chips.

3. **Shape** dough into 2 logs and transfer to baking sheet.

4. **Bake** for 20 minutes.

5. **Allow** to cool for 10 minutes. Slice, then return to oven for 5 minutes.

Recipe by
Mirel Freylich

Styling and photography by
Chay Berger

baked goods

Pumpkin Spice Buns

Pumpkin spice adds so much to everything. These buns are soft and delicious—perfect for a cold winter night.

Yield: 12 buns • dairy/pareve

DOUGH

2¾ cups	flour
3 Tbsp	sugar
4½ tsp	instant dry yeast
1 tsp	salt
½ cup	water
¼ cup	milk or non-dairy substitute
2 Tbsp	butter or margarine
1	egg

PUMPKIN SPICE MIXTURE

1 cup	pumpkin puree
½ cup	sugar
1 tsp	cinnamon
1 tsp	ginger
1 tsp	ground nutmeg
½	stick butter or margarine

CREAM CHEESE FROSTING

4 oz	cream cheese (or pareve alternative)
2½ cups	confectioners' sugar
1 Tbsp	milk

1. **Prepare the dough:** In a large bowl, mix flour, sugar, yeast, and salt.
2. **In** a microwave-safe bowl, combine water, milk, and butter or margarine and heat in a microwave for about 1 minute or until melted.
3. **Stir** milk mixture into the flour mixture. Add egg and mix for 3–4 minutes, until a dough forms. (It will be a bit sticky.)
4. **Grease** a bowl and place dough inside to rest while you prepare the pumpkin mixture.
5. **Preheat** oven to 200°F.
6. **Prepare the pumpkin spice mixture:** Place all ingredients in a bowl and mix well.
7. **Place** dough on a piece of parchment paper. Place another piece of parchment paper on top of the dough. Roll out to about 15 inches by 9 inches.
8. **Remove** the top parchment paper. Spread pumpkin spice mixture on the dough and roll up jelly-roll style.
9. **Using** a sharp knife, slice into 12 buns. Place buns in an 11x17-inch pan and cover tightly with foil.
10. **Turn** off the oven. Once oven is off for 10 minutes, put buns in. Allow them to sit in the oven for 15 minutes with the oven off.
11. **Remove** foil and bake at 375°F for 15–20 minutes.
12. **Remove** from oven and allow to cool.
13. **Prepare the frosting:** In a bowl, mix all ingredients together. Drizzle over buns.

Recipe by
Shaindy Siff

Styling and photography by
Chay Berger

baked goods

Berry-Yogurt Muffins

These are great to have in the freezer. Grab one on the way out or take the time to toast slightly before eating.

Yield: 12 muffins • dairy

1 cup plus 1 Tbsp	white whole wheat flour, divided
1 cup	quick oats
1 tsp	baking powder
1 tsp	baking soda
½ tsp	salt
1	egg
½ cup	oil
½ cup	Greek yogurt
½ cup	honey
1 tsp	vanilla
¾ cup	fresh or frozen berries

1. **Preheat** oven to 350°F. Grease or line muffin tins.

2. **In** a medium bowl, whisk together 1 cup flour, oats, baking powder, baking soda, and salt.

3. **In** a large bowl, combine egg, oil, yogurt, honey, and vanilla. Mix well. Slowly add the dry ingredients, ½ cup at a time, until just combined. Do not overmix.

4. **Toss** berries with 1 Tbsp flour. Fold berries into the batter.

5. **Fill** muffin tins ¾ of the way.

6. **Bake** for 20–25 minutes, until muffins are golden brown and an inserted toothpick comes out dry.

Recipe by
Shaindel Steinberg

Styling and photography by
Faigy Murray

baked goods

Chewy Peanut Butter Bars

The first time I made these bars, I asked everyone who tasted them to try to guess the mystery creamy ingredient. No one got it right. But everyone did agree that another batch needed to be made in the very near future!

Yield: 8 servings • pareve

1½ cups	salted and roasted peanuts, chopped
¾ cup	Medjool dates, pitted
6 Tbsp	honey
6 Tbsp	peanut butter
2 cups	quick oats
¼ cup	mini chocolate chips

1. **In** a food processor, pulse peanuts to chop into small pieces. Place nuts in a mixing bowl.

2. **Place** dates in the food processor and blend until smooth.

3. **Place** honey and peanut butter in a microwave-safe bowl and heat until smooth, about 1 minute on high. (Stop and stir during that time to make sure it doesn't overheat.) Alternatively, place ingredients in a saucepan and heat until melted together.

4. **Combine** with nuts, oats, and date puree.

5. **Press** into an 8x8-inch pan. Sprinkle chocolate chips on top and press down.

6. **Allow** to set and then cut into squares.

Recipe by
Nechama Norman

Styling and photography by
Esti Waldman

Oatmeal S'mores Bars

*Here's a fun twist on an old favorite.
Super-gooey and delicious!*

Yield: 8 servings • pareve

½ cup	oil
1 cup	brown sugar, packed
1	egg
2 tsp	vanilla extract
½ tsp	baking soda
Pinch	salt
1¼ cups	white whole wheat flour
1½ cups	quick oats
7-oz	jar marshmallow fluff
1 cup	mini chocolate chips

tip

Cut when semi-frozen for perfect slices.

Recipe by **Nechama Norman**
Styling and photography by **Esti Waldman**

1. **In** a mixer, cream oil and brown sugar until smooth. Beat in egg, vanilla, baking soda, and salt. Mix in flour, then slowly mix in oats.

2. **Line** an 8x8-inch pan with parchment paper. Press half the mixture into the bottom of the pan.

3. **Microwave** the jar of fluff for a few seconds–take it out just as the fluff starts rising out of the jar. Pour over the layer in the pan and spread evenly, taking care to leave a border around the edges with no marshmallow fluff.

4. **Sprinkle** chocolate chips over marshmallow fluff. Crumble remaining batter, covering all the edges with dough.

5. **Bake** at 350°F for 23–28 minutes, until the top is golden brown.

6. **Cool** completely before cutting.

Bourbon Walnut Cake

I tasted this delicious cake at a simcha and asked the hostess for the recipe. Then I tucked it into my notes but never actually did anything about it because it was such a patchke. But recently, I tried recreating the cake in an easier version. The result speaks for itself.

Yield: 1 Bundt pan • pareve

CAKE

- **1 cup** oil
- **1 cup** sugar
- **2** eggs
- **1 cup** orange juice
- **2 tsp** vanilla
- **4 cups** flour
- **2 tsp** baking powder

TOPPING

- **¼ cup** oil
- **¼ cup** brown sugar
- **½ cup** maple syrup
- **2 cups** walnuts, roughly chopped
- **1 tsp** vanilla

SAUCE

- **1 cup** maple syrup
- **½ cup** brown sugar
- **2 Tbsp** bourbon

1. **Preheat** oven to 350°F.

2. **In** a bowl, mix together cake ingredients.

3. **Grease** a Bundt pan and pour batter in.

4. **Combine** crumb ingredients. Sprinkle over the cake batter.

5. **Bake** for 35 minutes or until an inserted toothpick comes out clean.

6. **In** a small bowl, combine maple syrup, brown sugar and bourbon.

7. **Allow** cake to cool, then transfer to a serving plate. Using the flat end of a skewer, poke holes in the cake. Slowly pour the bourbon sauce over the cake, allowing it to seep into the holes.

tip

This can also be made in a 9x13-inch pan. Simply adjust baking time and check it after 25 minutes.

Recipe, styling, and photography by
Faigy Murray

baked goods

Ooey Gooey Monkey Bread

It's ooey, it's gooey, and it's sweet. It doesn't get any better than this!

Yield: 12 servings • pareve

2	20-oz packages pizza dough
1 cup	oil
1½ cups	sugar
½ cup	brown sugar
1½ Tbsp	cinnamon
½ tsp	nutmeg
	Oil spray

1. **Preheat** oven to 350°F.

2. **Roll** pizza dough into 1-inch balls and set aside.

3. **Pour** oil into a small bowl. In another bowl, mix sugars, cinnamon, and nutmeg.

4. **Spray** a Bundt pan very well with oil spray.

5. **Dip** dough balls into oil, then roll in the sugar mixture and lay in the pan.

6. **Once** the pan is full, bake for 45 minutes.

7. **Let** cool for 10 minutes before turning over.

8. **Serve** warm with ice cream.

Recipe by
Shaindy Siff

Styling and photography by
Faigy Murray

baked goods

Triple-Chip Hot Pies

This is the first step—and in my opinion the most important one—in creating the most delicious sundae. The combination of the hot pie with melting chips and cold ice cream is always a winner.

Yield: 10 pies • pareve

1½	sticks margarine, softened
¾ cup	sugar
¾ cup	brown sugar
3	eggs
1 tsp	vanilla sugar
2½ cups	flour
1 tsp	baking powder
⅓ cup	chocolate chips
⅓ cup	cappuccino chips
⅓ cup	caramel chips

1. **Preheat** oven to 350°F. Spray 10 ramekins with oil spray.

2. **In** the bowl of an electric mixer, cream margarine, sugar, and brown sugar. Add eggs, vanilla sugar, flour, and baking powder and mix until well combined. Mix in all chips.

3. **Press** dough into ramekins, filling about ⅔ of the way.

4. **Bake** for 22 minutes.

5. **Serve** warm.

Recipe by
Tova Lowenthal

Styling and photography by
Faigy Murray

baked goods

Maple Nut Cake

No more basic crumb cake! This one is delicious and different. Have a slice with a cup of coffee for the full experience.

Yield: 1 9x13-inch pan • dairy/pareve

2½ cups	flour
1 cup	brown sugar
½ tsp	salt
⅓ cup	butter or margarine
2 tsp	baking powder
½ tsp	baking soda
½ tsp	cinnamon
¼ tsp	ground nutmeg
2	eggs
1½ cups	milk or almond milk
½ cup	maple syrup
⅓ cup	applesauce
½ cup	chopped walnuts

1. **Preheat** oven to 350°F.

2. **In** a large bowl, combine flour, brown sugar, and salt. Add butter or margarine and mix until crumbly. Set aside ½ cup for topping.

3. **To** the bowl, add baking powder, baking soda, cinnamon, and nutmeg and mix until combined.

4. **In** a separate bowl, mix eggs, milk, maple syrup, and applesauce. Add wet mixture to the dry mixture and mix until combined.

5. **Pour** batter into a 9x13-inch pan. Sprinkle reserved crumbs on top, then sprinkle walnuts over the crumbs.

6. **Bake** for 40 minutes.

Recipe by
Shaindy Siff

Styling and photography by
Chay Berger

Zucchini Bread

Toast a slice and smear with butter—amazing!

Yield: 2 9-inch loaf pans • pareve

CAKE

3	eggs
2 cups	sugar
1 cup	oil
2 cups	shredded zucchini
3 cups	flour
½ tsp	baking soda
1 tsp	baking powder
1 tsp	cinnamon

TOPPING

1 cup	flour
1 cup	sugar
1	stick margarine or 4 Tbsp oil

1. **Preheat** oven to 350°F. Grease 2 loaf pans.

2. **Prepare the crumb topping:** Mix flour, sugar, and margarine or oil by hand until crumbs form.

3. **Prepare the cake:** Place eggs, sugar, oil, and zucchini in a mixing bowl. Mix for 5 minutes.

4. **In** a separate bowl, mix flour, baking soda, baking powder, and cinnamon. Slowly add to the wet mixture.

5. **Pour** batter into loaf pans and sprinkle crumbs on top.

6. **Bake** for 1 hour or until an inserted toothpick comes out clean.

Recipe by
Mirel Freylich

Styling and photography by
Chay Berger

baked goods

Egg-Free Fudgy Chocolate Cake

When I made this for the first time, I mistakenly omitted the eggs that the original recipe called for. I waited with bated breath to taste my flop, but it turned out delicious, fudgy, and moist!

Yield: 1 9x13-inch or Bundt pan • pareve

2 cups	boiling water
1 cup	oil
1 cup	cocoa
2½ cups	sugar
2 tsp	vanilla sugar
1 tsp	salt
2 tsp	baking soda
½ tsp	baking powder
3 cups	flour

1. **Preheat** oven to 350°F. Grease and flour a 9x13-inch or Bundt pan.

2. **In** the bowl of an electric mixer, combine water, oil, and cocoa. Add the rest of the ingredients and beat for 2 minutes until smooth.

3. **Pour** into pan and bake for 50–60 minutes or until an inserted toothpick comes out clean.

4. **Cool** and then frost with your favorite glaze or icing.

Recipe by
Nechama Norman

Styling and photography by
Faigy Murray

baked goods

Chex Bars

A yummy treat for the little ones, packed with all the goodies they love.

Yield: 1 9x13-inch pan • pareve

2½ cups	Chex cereal
3 cups	thin pretzel rods or mini pretzels
½ cup	unsalted margarine
½ cup	Peanut butter
10 oz	mini marshmallows
½ cup	chocolate chips

tip

These can be stored in an airtight container at room temperature for up to 1 week.

1. **Line** a 9x13-inch pan with foil and spray with baking spray for easier cleanup.

2. **In** a large bowl, place Chex and pretzels.

3. **In** a pot over medium heat, heat margarine and peanut butter. Mix until melted and smooth. Fold the marshmallows into the mixture.

4. **Pour** over the Chex and pretzels and mix well. Transfer into the prepared pan. Top with additional marshmallows and pretzels if desired.

5. **Melt** chocolate chips and drizzle over bars.

6. **Allow** bars to set fully before slicing and serving.

Recipe by
Sara Goldstein

Styling and photography by
Chay Berger

baked goods

cookie jar

Best Basic Cookies

With their combination of a soft yet crisp texture and big flavors, these cookies deliver on the promise of the ultimate comfort food: they satisfy. Variations are endless; your imagination is the limit.

Yield: 2–3 dozen cookies • pareve

1 cup	light or dark brown sugar, packed
½ cup	granulated sugar
2	large eggs
1 cup	canola or vegetable oil
1 Tbsp	pure vanilla extract
2 cups	all-purpose flour
1 cup	ground almonds
1 tsp	baking soda
½ tsp	salt
1 cup	desired fillers (see ideas below)

FLAVOR COMBINATION IDEAS

Classic chocolate chip: dark chocolate, roughly chopped

Oatmeal-raisin: rolled oats + raisins

Double chocolate: cocoa powder + chocolate, chopped

Peanut butter: peanut butter + peanuts, chopped

Chocolate-hazelnut: chocolate spread + hazelnuts, chopped

S'more: mini marshmallows + graham crackers, crushed + chocolate, chopped

Birthday cake: sprinkles + white chocolate chips

Klik: Klik chocolates, chopped

Lotus: lotus butter + lotus cookies, chopped

White chocolate-cranberry: white chocolate chips + dried cranberries

Chocolate speckled: cocoa powder + white chocolate chips

Colored candy: colorful chocolate lentils, Skittles, or Shneider's Rainballs

1. **Preheat** oven to 350° F. Line 2 baking sheets with parchment paper.

2. **In** the bowl of an electric mixer, beat sugars, eggs, oil, and vanilla until smooth.

3. **In** a separate bowl, combine flour, almonds, baking soda, and salt. Add flour mixture to the mixing bowl and mix. Add desired fillers and mix on the lowest speed until just combined.

4. **Form** balls and place on baking sheets, 2 inches apart.

5. **Bake** for 10–12 minutes, rotating pans halfway through.

6. **Cool** for 5 minutes, then transfer parchment paper onto wire racks to cool.

Do not overbake these cookies. They will look underbaked and mushy but will firm up as they cool.

If you don't like ground nuts in your cookies, replace with flour.

Recipe by
Dinah Bucholz

Styling and photography by
Chay Berger

cookie jar

Lemon Crinkle Cookies

In a tangy twist on the familiar crinkle cookie, the lemony flavor adds the perfect pizazz to this snow-coated treat. Let your teeth sink into these soft, fluffy, and creamy mini confections!

Yield: 2 dozen cookies • pareve

8-oz	container pareve cream cheese, softened
1	stick margarine, softened
1½ cups	sugar
2 Tbsp	lemon juice
⅛ tsp	yellow food coloring (optional, but it gives the cookies a bright, lemony look)
Pinch	salt
1	large egg plus 1 egg yolk
2½ cups	flour
2 tsp	baking powder
1 cup	confectioners' sugar

1. **In** the bowl of an electric mixer, mix cream cheese and margarine until smooth. Add sugar, lemon juice, food coloring, and salt and mix until fluffy (about 2 minutes). Add egg and the second yolk and beat until creamy.

2. **In** a small bowl, whisk flour and baking powder. Gradually add flour mixture to the mixer and mix on low speed until just incorporated.

3. **Cover** and refrigerate dough for 1–2 hours or overnight. (Alternatively, if you are short on time, you can add more flour.)

4. **Preheat** oven to 350°F. Line 2 baking sheets with parchment paper.

5. **Fill** a small bowl with confectioners' sugar.

6. **Shape** dough into even balls and roll in confectioners' sugar to coat. Place onto baking sheet, 1 inch apart.

7. **Bake** until cookies are puffed and crackly, about 13–14 minutes. The cookies will be soft in the center. If they start to brown at the edges, they have baked too long.

8. **Allow** to cool. Dust with confectioners' sugar before serving.

Recipe by
Faigy Stein

Styling and photography by
Chay Berger

cookie jar

Oatmeal Cookie Cups

The perfect breakfast to grab from the freezer in the morning.

Yield: 18 cookies • dairy

1½ cups	old-fashioned oats
1 cup	butter
1 cup	whole wheat flour
1 cup	white flour
1 cup	brown sugar
1 tsp	vanilla extract
1½ cups	strawberry jam

1. **Preheat** oven to 350°F. Grease muffin tins.

2. **In** a large bowl, place all ingredients besides strawberry jam. Using your hands, mix until fully combined.

3. **Press** half the batter into muffin tins. Top each one with 1 tsp strawberry jam. Press the remaining batter on top, making sure the sides meet.

4. **Bake** for 15–20 minutes, until browned.

5. **Allow** to cool for 10 minutes before transferring to a wire rack.

Recipe by
Shaindy Siff

Styling and photography by
Chay Berger

cookie jar

Peanut Butter Streusel Cookies

These soft, buttery delights are the perfect blend of peanut butter flavor and crumbly streusel topping.

Yield: 2 dozen cookies • pareve

COOKIES

1	stick margarine
¾ cup	peanut butter
1½ tsp	vanilla extract
½ cup	brown sugar
½ cup	sugar
⅛ tsp	salt
½ tsp	baking powder
1½ cups	flour
2	eggs

STREUSEL TOPPING

¼ cup	flour
¼ cup	brown sugar
1 Tbsp	sugar
½ tsp	cinnamon
¼ cup	peanut butter
1 Tbsp	margarine, melted

GLAZE

½ cup	peanut butter

1. **Preheat** oven to 350°F.

2. **Prepare the cookie dough:** In the bowl of an electric mixer, beat margarine, peanut butter, and vanilla extract. Add sugars, salt, and baking powder. Gradually add flour. Continue mixing until well incorporated. Beat in eggs, one at a time.

3. **Roll** dough into 1½-inch balls. Flatten slightly with a fork, making a crisscross.

4. **Prepare the streusel:** In a bowl, whisk flour, sugars, and cinnamon. Add peanut butter and mix with a fork. Add melted margarine and mix until mixture is crumbly. If needed, add more margarine or flour to make it more crumbly.

5. **Lightly** press streusel onto cookies.

6. **Bake** for 10–13 minutes. Allow to cool completely before glazing.

7. **Prepare the glaze:** Melt peanut butter. Drizzle over cookies.

Recipe by
Faigy Stein

Styling and photography by
Chay Berger

cookie jar

Turtle Cookies

These picture-perfect, mouthwatering miniatures are a great way to enhance any simcha. Bring on the joy!

Yield: 10–12 cookies • pareve

COOKIES

½ cup	brown sugar
1	stick margarine
¼ tsp	vanilla sugar
1	egg plus 1 egg yolk
1½ cups	flour
¼ tsp	baking soda

GLAZE

⅓ cup	chocolate chips
3 Tbsp	pareve milk or coffee creamer
1 Tbsp	margarine
1 cup	confectioners' sugar

TOPPING

1 cup	pecan halves

1. **Preheat** oven to 350°F. Line a baking sheet with parchment paper.

2. **Prepare the cookie dough:** In the bowl of an electric mixer, beat brown sugar and margarine until light and fluffy. Add vanilla sugar, egg, and egg yolk and beat well. Stir in flour and baking soda. Mix well.

3. **Form** 1-inch balls and place on baking sheet.

4. **Bake** for 10–12 minutes or until edges are golden brown. Allow to cool.

5. **Prepare the glaze:** In a small pot over low heat, melt chocolate chips, pareve milk or creamer, and margarine, stirring constantly until mixture is melted and smooth.

6. **Remove** from heat and add confectioners' sugar. If the mixture is too watery, add more confectioners' sugar to thicken.

7. **Frost** the cooled cookies with the glaze. Top each cookie with a pecan half.

Recipe by
Faigy Stein

Styling by
Atara Schechter

Photography by
Ruby Studios

cookie jar

Sandwich Cookies

Combining these jumbo melt-in-your-mouth cookies with a creamy filling makes for a dream cookie.

Yield: 9 large sandwich cookies • pareve

COOKIES

4 cups	flour
2 sticks	margarine
2	eggs
½ tsp	salt
1½ cups	sugar
1 tsp	baking powder
1 Tbsp	vanilla sugar
¼ cup	orange juice

FILLING

½ stick	margarine
8 oz	pareve cream cheese
3 cups	confectioners' sugar

TOPPING

3.5-oz	bar baking chocolate

1. **Preheat** oven to 350°F. Line a baking sheet with parchment paper.

2. **Prepare the cookie dough:** In the bowl of an electric mixer, beat flour and margarine until combined. Add eggs and salt and mix. Add the rest of the ingredients and combine to form a smooth dough.

3. **Measure** 3½ Tbsp dough and form into a ball. Place onto baking sheet and flatten. Repeat with remaining dough. Note: You can use less dough to create smaller cookies.

4. **Bake** for 15 minutes. Allow to cool.

5. **Prepare the filling:** In the bowl of an electric mixer, beat filling ingredients.

6. **Place** the filling in a pastry bag fitted with a large star tip. Pipe cream on the flat side of half of the cookies. Top each one with another cookie to create a sandwich. Freeze the cookies for 2 hours.

7. **Prepare the topping:** Melt chocolate. Dip one side of each frozen cookie into chocolate. Allow the excess chocolate to drip off and place upright on a sheet of parchment paper, with the chocolate on a diagonal, to harden.

Recipe by
Faigy Stein

Styling by
Atara Schechter

Photography by
Ruby Studios

cookie jar

Lemon Meringue Mini Cookie Pies

These delicious mini pies make a tangy, sweet treat for a special occasion.

Yield: 15 cookies • pareve

MERINGUES

4	egg whites
¼ tsp	salt
¼ tsp	cream of tartar (optional)
1 cup	sugar

COOKIES

1 stick	unsalted margarine
¼ cup	sugar
1½ cups	flour
⅛ tsp	salt
1	large egg yolk
2 Tbsp	whip topping

LEMON CURD

4	egg yolks
¾ cup	sugar
6 Tbsp	freshly squeezed lemon juice
4 Tbsp	margarine

1. **Prepare the meringues:** Preheat oven to 225°F. Line 2 baking sheets with parchment paper.

2. **In** the bowl of an electric mixer, beat egg whites until foamy. Add salt and cream of tartar. Slowly add sugar, 1 Tbsp at a time. Keep mixing on high until a very stiff meringue forms (about 5 minutes).

3. **Place** the meringue into a plastic piping bag fitted with a large star tip (or the Sultan tip, available on Amazon). Hold the bag about ½ inch above the parchment paper and pipe the meringues. If you are using a regular star tip, use your thumb to create a round imprint on each meringue.

4. **Bake** meringues for 1 hour and 45 minutes to 2 hours.

5. **Prepare the cookies:** Preheat oven to 350°F.

6. **In** a food processor fitted with the S-blade, pulse the margarine and sugar just until the sugar disappears. Add flour and salt and pulse again until margarine is crumbly.

7. **In** a small bowl, mix egg yolk and whip topping. Add mixture to the food processor and pulse to incorporate. The dough will be crumbly.

8. **On** a piece of parchment paper, roll the dough to ¼ inch thickness. Place parchment paper onto baking sheet and refrigerate for about 1 hour.

9. **Cut** the dough into 3-inch circles (slightly larger than the meringues). Bake for 12–15 minutes.

10. **Prepare the lemon curd:** In a medium-sized pot, place yolks and sugar and beat with a fork to blend. Stir in lemon juice and margarine. Cook over medium heat, stirring constantly, until the mixture thickens. It should coat the back of a spoon but still be liquid enough to pour. Do not allow to boil or it will curdle.

11. **When** the mixture has thickened, pour it into a sifter and sift.

12. **Place** plastic wrap on top and allow to cool.

13. **Assemble:** Place a meringue on top of each cookie. Using a spoon or piping bag, fill the center of the meringue with lemon curd.

note

These cookies should be stored in the refrigerator, not the freezer, since meringues melt when defrosted.

tip

To check if a meringue is ready, try to lift it. If it comes off the pan smoothly and the bottom is dry, it is done. If it is not separating easily and the bottom is still sticky, return to the oven.

Recipe by **Faigy Stein**
Styling and photography by **Chay Berger**

cookie jar

healthy eats

Peanut Butter Cups

The perfect recipe for the perfect sweet (with just a hint of saltiness) for when you want to treat yourself in a healthy way.

Yield: 12 cups • pareve

CHOCOLATE MIXTURE

8 oz good-quality dark chocolate (at least 60 percent cacao)

2 Tbsp all-natural peanut butter

PEANUT BUTTER FILLING

1 cup all-natural peanut butter

⅓ cup pure maple syrup or honey

¼ cup almond flour

Sea salt flakes (optional)

1. **Prepare the chocolate mixture:** Place chocolate and peanut butter in a microwave-safe bowl and melt in the microwave for 1½ minutes in 30-second increments, mixing after each 30 seconds.

2. **Prepare the peanut butter filling:** In a bowl, mix ingredients by hand until smooth. (You may need to add more flour.)

3. **Assemble:** Line cupcake holders. Place 1–2 tsp chocolate mixture in the bottom of each liner. Place 1 Tbsp peanut butter mixture on top of the chocolate and press to flatten if needed. Top with 1–2 more tsp chocolate mixture. Sprinkle sea salt if desired.

4. **Place** in the freezer for 30–45 minutes, until solid. Store in the refrigerator.

Recipe by
Shaindel Steinberg

Styling and photography by
Chana Rivky Klein

healthy eats

Baked Oatmeal

The perfect cross between a muffin and a bowl of oatmeal—not quite as dry as a muffin but not as wet as oatmeal. This recipe works best made in small ramekins or hard cupcake holders.

Yield: 6–8 servings • dairy/pareve

1½ cups	quick-cooking oats
¾ cup	milk or almond milk
2	eggs
¾ cup	applesauce
2 Tbsp	maple syrup or honey
2 Tbsp	peanut butter
¾ tsp	baking powder
1 tsp	cinnamon
½ cup	mini chocolate chips
¼ cup	peanut butter

1. **Preheat** oven to 350°F. Grease muffin tins or ramekins.

2. **In** a food processor fitted with the S-blade, blend oatmeal until almost flour-like. Add the rest of the ingredients except the chocolate chips and peanut butter and blend until smooth and creamy.

3. **Pour** into muffin tins or ramekins. Sprinkle chocolate chips on top.

4. **Bake** for 25 minutes.

5. **Melt** peanut butter and drizzle over muffins.

Recipe, styling, and photography by
Faigy Murray

healthy eats

Roasted Veggie Lasagna

A delicious and satisfying healthier take on lasagna which freezes beautifully and takes just a few minutes to heat up. Paired with a fresh salad, it will keep you feeling full for a long time.

Yield: 4 servings • dairy

2	eggplants, thinly sliced lengthwise
½ tsp	kosher salt
2	large zucchini, thinly sliced lengthwise
26-oz	jar marinara sauce
16-oz	container low-fat cottage cheese
½ tsp	black pepper
2	garlic cloves, crushed, or frozen garlic cubes
2 cups	shredded cheese

1. **Sprinkle** kosher salt over eggplant slices. Place eggplant and zucchini slices on paper towels for 30 minutes.

2. **Meanwhile,** in a medium bowl, mix marinara sauce, cottage cheese, pepper, and garlic until combined.

3. **Preheat** oven to 400°F. Line a baking sheet with parchment paper and spray with oil spray.

4. **Blot** the vegetables with a paper towel to remove the moisture that was released. Place veggies on the prepared pan and roast in the oven for 20 minutes. Flip and roast for another 10–15 minutes, until golden brown. Remove from oven and cool.

5. **Lower** oven temperature to 350°F.

6. **In** a 9x13-inch pan or 4 loaf pans, pour ¼ of the sauce and top with a layer of roasted zucchini, then ½ cup shredded cheese, and finally a layer of eggplant. Repeat the layers 2 more times until all the eggplant and zucchini slices are used. Top with remaining sauce and then cheese.

7. **Spray** a sheet of foil with oil spray and use it to cover the lasagna. Bake for 45 minutes. Uncover and bake for another 10–15 minutes, until cheese is bubbly.

8. **Remove** lasagna from oven and let sit for at least 45 minutes to firm up. Enjoy at room temperature, or freeze and reheat uncovered at 350°F for 15–20 minutes.

Recipe by
Shaindel Steinberg

Styling and photography by
Chay Berger

healthy eats

Almond Flour Schnitzel

This makes a delicious, easy supper. Serve with Israeli salad and some homemade sweet potato fries and you've got yourself a healthy meal which the whole family can enjoy.

Yield: 6–8 servings • meat

1½ cups	almond flour
1 tsp	salt
Dash	black pepper
2 tsp	garlic powder
2 tsp	paprika
2 tsp	smoked paprika
2	eggs
8–10	chicken cutlets, thinly sliced
	Avocado oil spray

1. **Preheat** oven to 400°F. Line a baking sheet with parchment paper.

2. **Combine** almond flour and spices. Lightly beat eggs. Dip chicken in egg and then in almond flour mixture.

3. **Place** breaded chicken on baking sheet and spray with avocado oil. Bake for 20 minutes or until the chicken has a nice color and bottoms are crispy. Alternatively, you can pan-fry your chicken in avocado oil.

Recipe by
Odaiah Leeds

Styling by
Atara Schechter

Photography by
Ruby Studios

healthy eats

Free Soup

The perfect soup which will fill your stomach and warm you without the added fats and carbs. I call it the Free Soup because you can eat as much as you want of it...it's only good for you!

Yield: 12 servings • pareve

	Oil spray
1	onion, diced
1 Tbsp plus ⅛ tsp	salt, divided
2	garlic cloves or frozen garlic cubes
1	parsnip, sliced
1	carrot, sliced
2	stalks celery, sliced
1 pint	mushrooms, sliced
1	small turnip, diced
1	small celery knob, diced
6–8 cups	water
15-oz	can crushed or diced tomatoes
1 tsp	black pepper
3	frozen dill cubes
⅛ tsp	cayenne pepper (optional)

1. **Place** a large pot on the stove over medium heat and spray with oil spray. Add onion and ⅛ tsp salt. Sauté for 3–4 minutes, until translucent. Add garlic and sauté for 2–3 minutes, until fragrant.

2. **Lower** heat to medium-low. Add the rest of the vegetables and sauté for 30 minutes.

3. **Add** water to cover the vegetables by 2 inches. Add tomatoes.

4. **Bring** to a boil and season with salt and pepper. Lower to a simmer and cook for 2–3 hours. Add dill and cayenne pepper and simmer for another 15 minutes.

Recipe by
Shaindel Steinberg

Styling and photography by
Chay Berger

healthy eats

Fudgy Peanut Chew-Date Balls

I love having a healthy dessert option stocked in my freezer. These date balls make an amazing sweet treat.

Yield: 2 dozen balls • pareve

24	large, juicy Medjool dates
⅓ cup	water
½ cup	almond butter
¼ cup	peanut butter
3 Tbsp	cocoa powder
1 tsp	vanilla extract (optional)

1. **Place** dates in a food processor fitted with the S-blade. Process until a smooth, pasty consistency forms. Slowly add water as needed.

2. **Add** almond butter, peanut butter, cocoa powder, and vanilla extract and process until just blended together. Don't overprocess.

3. **Wet** your hands or gloves and form balls.

4. **Keep** in the freezer until you're ready to eat. Consistency should stay soft and fudgy even when frozen.

Recipe by
Odaiah Leeds

Styling and photography by
Chay Berger

Smoothie Bowl

Refreshing, filling, and topped with delicious crunch, a smoothie bowl is the perfect mini meal or healthy snack for the busy woman (or teenager). Since I started making these at home, not only can I have them all the time, but I can also customize them to my taste.

Yield: 1 serving • dairy/pareve

SMOOTHIE

1 cup frozen banana or pineapple

1 cup frozen berries or pitaya (dragon fruit)

⅛ avocado (optional)

¼ cup milk or orange juice

1 Tbsp acai powder (optional)

TOPPINGS (choose one, some, or all)

Almond butter

Fresh sliced fruit

Toasted nuts

Shredded coconut

Granola

Frozen berries

Mini chocolate chips

Fresh figs

Dried dates

1. **Place** smoothie ingredients in a blender and blend until smooth. If too thick, add more liquid, 1 Tbsp at a time. Keep blending for 5 minutes, until mixture is light and smooth.

2. **Pour** into a bowl and top with desired toppings.

Recipe by
Shaindel Steinberg

Styling and photography by
Chay Berger

healthy eats

Meat Pizza

One of my favorite things to do is take seemingly unhealthy recipes and elevate them.
This meat pizza is restaurant-worthy but still made with quality ingredients. It is grain
free and refined-sugar free but packed with so much amazing flavor.

Yield: 6 servings • meat

PULLED BEEF

1	onion, sliced
1.5–2-lb	second-cut brisket or top-of-the-rib roast
1 cup	tomato sauce
½ cup	coconut aminos
2 tsp	garlic powder
1 tsp	salt
1 tsp	paprika
1 tsp	smoked paprika
Dash	black pepper

FLATBREAD CRUST

2 cups	almond flour*
1 cup	arrowroot*
½ cup	coconut flour*
½ cup	tapioca starch*
1 cup	warm water
¼ tsp	salt
2 Tbsp	oil

*If you can't find these starches and flours at your local supermarket, you can use 4 cups of any healthy flour blend you like.

TOMATO JAM

6	Roma tomatoes
⅛ cup	honey
1½ Tbsp	apple cider vinegar
Pinch	salt

CASHEW-GARLIC "MAYO"

1 cup	cashews
½ cup	water
½ tsp	salt
Dash	black pepper
1	head of garlic, roasted
	Juice of ½ lemon

GARNISH (OPTIONAL)

Caramelized onions

Arugula or other fresh greens of choice

1. **Prepare the pulled beef:** Place onion slices on the bottom of a 9x13-inch pan. Place meat on top of onions.

2. **In** a bowl, combine tomato sauce, coconut aminos, and spices. Pour over meat.

3. **Cover** tightly and bake at 300°F until meat is fork tender (approximately 4–5 hours). Using 2 forks, shred the beef.

4. **Prepare the flatbread crust:** In a large bowl, mix all ingredients together until a dough forms.

tip

This step can be done in advance and the dough can be kept frozen until ready to use.

5. **Line** a baking sheet with parchment paper. Roll out dough evenly on the pan. Shape the dough into 2 long rectangular flatbreads.

6. **Bake** at 400°F for 10–12 minutes or until the dough is golden and crispy around the edges.

7. **Prepare the tomato jam:** In a pot, combine ingredients and bring to a boil. Simmer on low for 40–60 minutes. Mash with a fork and let cool.

8. **Prepare the cashew-garlic mayo:** Soak cashews in water for 30 minutes. Drain and rinse cashews. Place all mayo ingredients in a high-power blender or a food processor fitted with the S-blade and blend until smooth and creamy.

9. **Assemble:** Spread tomato jam on the flatbreads, then add pulled beef and caramelized onions if using. (If you will need to rewarm it, stop here and add the rest after warming.) Top with arugula and drizzle with cashew-garlic mayo.

Recipe by **Odaiah Leeds**
Styling by **Atara Schechter**
Photography by **Ruby Studios**

healthy eats

Techinah-Infused Muffins

Yield: 14 medium-sized muffins • pareve

½ cup	honey
⅓ cup	tahini paste
¼ cup	water
2	eggs
¼ cup	orange juice
1 tsp	baking soda
1 tsp	baking powder
1 cup	whole wheat flour
¼ cup	chocolate chips (optional)

1. **Preheat** oven to 350°F. Line muffin tins.

2. **In** the bowl of an electric mixer, place all ingredients in order, mixing on low speed.

3. **Pour** batter into 14 muffin holders and bake for 14 minutes.

Recipe by
Mirel Freylich

Styling and photography by
Faigy Murray

healthy eats

Baked Apple Chips

Whenever I smell these chips baking, I wonder why I don't make them more often. They are super-crisp and taste like fall with their cinnamon-sugar topping. Perfect for a yummy, healthy back-to-school snack!

Yield: **2 cups** • pareve

2	apples, sliced ¼ inch thick with a mandoline or sharp knife
	Canola oil spray
1 Tbsp	sugar
½ tsp	cinnamon

1. **Preheat** oven to 200°F. Line 2 baking sheets with parchment paper.

2. **Spread** apple slices onto baking sheets and spray generously with oil spray.

3. **In** a bowl, mix sugar and cinnamon. Sprinkle evenly over apple slices.

4. **Bake** for 2 hours or more as needed, until apple slices are crisp.

5. **Remove** chips from oven and let cool completely before transferring to a container. Chips remain fresh for up to 3 days in a sealed container.

Recipe by
Sara Goldstein

Styling and photography by
Faigy Murray

healthy eats

Rainbow Quinoa Bowl

Magnificent color, taste, and texture blend together in this wonder dish.

Yield: 2 servings • pareve

QUINOA

¾ cup	quinoa
1½ cups	water
1 tsp	oil

SWEET POTATO

1	sweet potato, peeled and cubed
2 Tbsp	oil
¼ tsp	salt
¼ tsp	pepper

BEETS

1	beet, peeled and sliced into half rings
2 tsp	oil

1	avocado, sliced into half rings
4	radishes, sliced
½ cup	edamame, cooked

DRESSING

3 Tbsp	olive oil
1 tsp	lemon juice
¼ tsp	salt
Dash	black pepper

1. **Preheat** oven to 350°F.

2. **Place** quinoa ingredients in a baking pan and stir. Bake covered for 40 minutes.

3. **Line** a baking sheet with parchment paper.

4. **In** a medium-sized bowl, combine sweet potato ingredients. Spread onto baking sheet. Add beets alongside sweet potato and drizzle with oil. Bake for 15 minutes.

5. **Place** quinoa in 2 bowls and cover with remaining ingredients except dressing. Add dressing ingredients and toss gently prior to serving.

Recipe, styling, and photography by
Mirel Freylich

healthy eats

Healthier Granola

This healthy granola is a family favorite. When made into bars, it makes a great grab-and-go breakfast option or an awesome after-school snack.

Yield: 18 servings • pareve

½ cup plus
1 Tbsp ground flaxseed, divided
3 Tbsp water
2 cups old-fashioned oats
1 cup almond flour
¼ cup avocado oil
¾ cup honey
2 tsp vanilla extract
Pinch salt
¾ tsp cinnamon
¾ cup chocolate chips

1. **Line** a baking sheet (or a 9x13-inch pan, for bars) with parchment paper.

2. **Combine** 1 Tbsp ground flaxseed with water, mix, and let it sit. This is your flax egg.

3. **In** a bowl, combine remaining ingredients. Add the flax egg.

4. **Press** mixture into pan.

5. **Bake** at 350°F for 30 minutes.

6. **For** granola, break up into small pieces. For bars, let it sit for 5 minutes before slicing.

Recipe by
Odaiah Leeds

Styling and photography by
Chay Berger

The Taste of Our Traditions

Yitti Berkovic

When my grandmother was already in her 80s, although it was hard for her to walk and to hear, she still had an adventurous streak.

Small, frail, but always spirited, she called me over at my cousin's *vort* and gestured toward the buffet with a wink. "I'd like to try a piece of sushi."

I laughed out loud.

Back then, sushi was relatively new to the kosher scene, and everyone else in her age group had spurned the Japanese-but-suddenly-*heimish* delicacy as the "latest *meshuga'as*" unworthy of its place on the table.

But Bobby, not even five feet tall, had eyes that sparkled with humor and wit and joie de vivre. A Holocaust survivor, she embraced America as a *medinah shel chessed* and enjoyed the gifts and freedoms her new homeland had to offer, including pizza, ice cream, and hot dogs with mustard.

In her own home, at her own table, she served her husband, my *zeidy*, the tastes of the *alter heim*: chicken *gargalach* (necks), borscht, kugels, and radishes. For us, the grandchildren whom she loved to spoil, she always had some all-American treats stashed in her narrow pantry—chocolate bars, bialys, and homemade sugar cookies—but the flavors of her home were Hungarian delicacies, foods I struggled to pronounce, let alone spell.

So I was more than a little surprised when she wanted to try sushi, a food as foreign to her as *aranygaluska* was to me.

"Are you sure, Bobby?"

She waved away my hesitation and insisted with her sweet Slovakian lilt, "I want to see what all the excitement is about."

I played along, but I tried to go easy on her, choosing an inoffensive salmon avocado roll and keeping the wasabi off her plate. I also encouraged her to use a fork instead of chopsticks and to eschew the spicy mayo for the less intimidating soy sauce.

By the time she was ready to bite into her piece, she was surrounded by a squad of cheering grandchildren, eager to see Bobby's reaction to a food she'd never tasted.

Her eyes dancing, she raised her piece of sushi in the air like she was offering a *l'chaim* and then took her first bite. Immediately, her forehead creased.

"I don't understand it," she sputtered. "This is what costs so much money? It has no taste!"

We burst out laughing, and I hurried to bring her a piece of hot potato kugel instead.

"Now this," she announced with a sniff, "is delicious and worth every penny!"

Years have gone by since Bobby passed away, and I miss her fiercely. I miss the way her smile lit up every corner of her face, and I miss the way she injected love and humor into every conversation. And when I see sushi stations at *simcha* after *simcha*, in pizza shops and high-end *fleishig*

restaurants, I picture the bewilderment on her face and I hear her laughter, her gentle way of letting us know she thought we were all crazy to eat the things we ate those days.

Truth is, she wouldn't recognize so many of the foods that now make their way to my Shabbos table or that fill the pages of this cookbook. If sushi left her befuddled, what would she say about the meat pizzas and sourdough bread and charcuterie boards that are so popular as this book goes to print?

She, who loved a cucumber salad with just Kirbies and onions, what would she say to my salads, dotted with avocado and mango, jalapeño peppers and kale?

She, who painstakingly made gefilte fish and carp from scratch, what would she say to my Moroccan salmon and herbed branzino and seared tuna steaks?

I can just picture her bewilderment at the foods of the future that haven't yet made it into Jewish homes but will soon be all the rage.

The delicacies she once prided herself on serving—the *shmaltz*, the livers, the crispy fried chicken skins—they have fallen out of style among her granddaughters, who pride themselves on cooking with a more cosmopolitan flair. Our tables do not reflect her *alter heim* alone; we have also absorbed the flavors of our fellow Jews who have walked different paths.

The road Klal Yisrael has traveled is long and winding, crisscrossing con-

tinents and cultures and cuisines. I may come from my grandmother's Hungarian, Ashkenazic heritage, but I swap recipes with friends who hail from Sephardic origins, from Morocco and from Syria, from Israel in her earliest days. I swap recipes with friends who were also taught by their grandmothers to cook with love and joy and generosity.

So Bobby would laugh and look on in confusion at my dip bowls filled with hummus and guacamole and sriracha. She would marvel at my Yom Tov menus that include lamb riblets, shawarma, and spicy matbucha, hardly staples of the *shtetl*. She'd ask, "Where is the compote?" and "What's wrong with some sponge cake?" if I offered her one of my elaborate desserts.

But I'd also like to think that she'd feel right at home at my table, even if I don't prepare the chicken necks she served as proudly as I'd serve an aged steak. Because she would understand that the flavors of our foods, the seasonings of our sustenance, may vary with the times, influenced by the changes happening around us, but some things won't ever change.

Because Bobby and I, we cook with the same ingredients: Love. Worry. A desire for our children to be healthy and happy and strong.

Even if our spice cabinets diverge, we cook for the same reasons: we cook to feed others. We cook to show our husband and our children that we value their health and well-being (and their picky preferences). We cook to make our Shabbos and Yom Tov tables warm and inviting and nourishing for our families and our guests, for our bodies and our souls.

So, if she came for a meal today (oh, how I wish she could!), Bobby might be surprised by the flavors on my table. Still, I know she'd be endlessly proud of whatever foods I've prepared. Because our differing menus reflect the journey our nation has taken, but they also reflect the path from which we will never veer.

yamim tovim

Vibrant Simanim Salad

This bold, fresh mix will enhance your simanim table.

Yield: 4–6 servings • pareve

SALAD

2 cups	shredded purple cabbage
1 cup	shredded carrot
1	mango, diced
½ cup	pomegranate seeds
3	scallions, chopped

DRESSING

1 Tbsp	oil
1 Tbsp	brown sugar
1 Tbsp	lemon juice
1 tsp	orange juice

1. **Place** all salad ingredients in a salad bowl.

2. **In** a small bowl, combine dressing ingredients. Pour over salad prior to serving and toss.

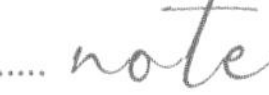

note

You can add in cooked, shredded beets, but the salad will lose its vibrancy when their deep color bleeds.

Recipe by
Mirel Freylich

Styling and photography by
Chay Berger

Glazed Cinnamon-Apple Wontons

This dessert is the perfect complement to your Rosh Hashanah menu. It's super-simple to prepare and delicious too!

Yield: 4 servings • pareve

3	Granny Smith apples, peeled, cored, and cut into wedges
3 Tbsp	margarine
⅛ cup	sugar plus more for sprinkling
⅛ cup	brown sugar
1 Tbsp	flour
1 Tbsp	lemon juice
1 tsp	cinnamon
Pinch	nutmeg
8	mini wonton wrappers
	Oil spray
	Confectioners' sugar, for sprinkling

1. **Preheat** oven to 250°F.

2. **Place** apples in a pan. Add margarine, sugar, brown sugar, flour, lemon juice, cinnamon, and nutmeg and toss to coat. Cover and bake for 1 hour and 15 minutes.

3. **Raise** oven temperature to 375°F. Line a baking sheet with parchment paper.

4. **Place** wonton wrappers on baking sheet. Sprinkle with sugar and spray with oil spray. Bake for 5 minutes or until golden brown.

5. **Assemble:** Lay a spoonful of warm apple mixture on each wonton and sprinkle with confectioners' sugar. Serve with vanilla ice cream.

Recipe by
Chaya Ruchie Schwartz

Styling and photography by
Faigy Murray

rosh hashanah

Silan-Glazed Colored Carrots

The striking colors in this simanim-themed side will truly impress.

Yield: 4–6 servings • pareve

2.5 lb	carrots in assorted colors (orange, yellow, white, purple)
2 Tbsp	silan
2 Tbsp	oil
1 tsp	soy sauce
½ tsp	garlic powder
¼ tsp	pepper

note

Use equal amounts of all colors except purple. Use half the amount of purple since the color bleeds.

1. **Preheat** oven to 375°F.

2. **Peel** carrots without removing the stems. Wash well and pat dry. Place in a 9x13-inch pan.

3. **In** a small bowl, whisk remaining ingredients together. Slowly pour over carrots, rubbing until fully coated.

4. **Cover** and bake for 40 minutes. Uncover and bake for an additional 15 minutes.

Recipe by
Mirel Freylich

Styling and photography by
Chay Berger

rosh hashanah

Spiced Apple Cider

While this is not a "from scratch" recipe for authentic apple cider, it's a really delicious cheat.

Yield: 6 cups • pareve

6 cups	apple juice
¼ cup	maple syrup
2	cinnamon sticks plus more for garnish
½ tsp	vanilla
1	orange, sliced (optional)

1. **In** a large pot over medium heat bring all ingredients to a gentle boil for 30 minutes. Reduce heat to low and simmer for another 30 minutes.

2. **Remove** orange slices and cinnamon sticks. Serve each cup with a fresh cinnamon stick for garnish.

Recipe by
Nechama Norman

Styling and photography by
FP Photography

sukkos

Flanken-Mushroom-Barley Soup

This warm, filling soup just right for those cold Sukkos nights in the sukkah.

Yield: 8 servings • meat

2 lb	flanken meat, cut into chunks
2 Tbsp	oil
1	onion, diced
20 oz	fresh mushrooms, sliced
4	cloves garlic, minced
2	marrow bones (optional)
¾ cups	barley
4 cups	beef stock
5 cups	water
	Salt
	Black pepper

1. **In** a large pot, brown meat for about 5 minutes. Set aside.

2. **Sauté** onion, mushrooms, and garlic in oil until soft. Return meat to the pot and add remaining ingredients.

3. **Simmer** for 3–4 hours, stirring occasionally.

Recipe by
Shaindy Siff

Styling and photography by
Faigy Murray

sukkos

Warm Berry Tea Trifle

The compote sauce is delicious when served warm, but feel free to serve it cold too.

Yield: 6 mini trifle cups • pareve

POUND CAKE

6	eggs
2 cups	sugar
1 cup	oil
2 cups	flour
1 tsp	baking powder
2 tsp	vanilla sugar
1 package	instant vanilla pudding
1 cup	orange juice

WHIP

8 oz	whip topping
½ package	instant vanilla pudding

BERRY TEA COMPOTE

2	peaches, pitted and sliced
1½ cups	frozen blueberries, plus more for garnish
¼ cup	water
2 tsp	lemon juice
¼ cup	sugar
2	limonana tea bags
2 tsp	cornstarch dissolved in
1 Tbsp	water
Dash	cinnamon

1. **Prepare the cake:** Preheat oven to 350°F. Grease a 9x13-inch pan.

2. **Beat** eggs and sugar until pale yellow and fluffy. Add the rest of the ingredients and mix until incorporated.

3. **Pour** into pan and bake for 45 minutes to 1 hour, until an inserted toothpick comes out clean.

4. **Prepare the whip:** In the bowl of an electric mixer, beat whip topping and pudding until stiff.

5. **Prepare the compote:** In a medium pot, place all compote ingredients and cook for 10 minutes.

6. **Assemble:** In trifle cups, layer cake and some compote. Top with a dollop of whip. Garnish with berries.

tip

You can use store-bought sponge cake with great results.

note

It's best to assemble these right before serving s the compote can be kept warm.

Recipe by
Chaya Ruchie Schwartz

Styling and photography by
Chana Rivky Klein

sukkos

Potato Dreidel Stacks

I love to get into the Yom Tov spirit! This is my spin on potato bourekas, Chanukah style.

Yield: 10 servings • pareve

DREIDELS

20 pastry dough squares

Oil spray

POTATO FILLING

10 Yukon Gold potatoes, peeled and quartered

Water

Salt

2 frozen garlic cubes

¾ stick margarine

Pepper

MUSHROOM SAUCE

16 oz fresh mushrooms, sliced

1 large white onion, diced

2 frozen garlic cubes

½ Tbsp chicken soup mix

2 Tbsp white cooking wine

2 Tbsp oil

Salt to taste

Black pepper to taste

1½ Tbsp cornstarch dissolved in
1½ Tbsp water

1. **Preheat** oven to 350°F. Line a baking sheet with parchment paper.

2. **Prepare the dreidels:** Using a dreidel-shaped cookie cutter, cut a dreidel out of each pastry square. Using a fork, poke some holes in the dough. Oil-spray each dreidel. Bake for 20 minutes, until golden.

3. **Prepare the potatoes:** Place potatoes in a pot and fill with water to cover. Add salt. Cook on medium-high heat for 20–30 minutes, until soft.

4. **Once** cooked, drain potatoes and pour them back into the pot. Add garlic, margarine, salt, and pepper. Using a fork or potato masher, mash until smooth.

5. **Prepare the mushroom sauce:** In a large frying pan, combine mushrooms, onions, garlic, chicken soup mix, white wine, oil, salt, and pepper. Sauté on medium-low for 15–20 minutes, until soft. Add cornstarch and bring to a boil. Once sauce has thickened, lower flame until ready to eat.

6. **Assemble:** Place one dreidel on a plate. Using a piping bag, pipe potato mixture onto the dreidel. Place another dreidel on top. Pour mushrooms sauce on top. Repeat with remaining dreidels.

Recipe by **Shaindy Siff**
Styling and photography by **Chay Berger**

chanukah

Yapchik Latkes

Upgrade your standard potato latke to something truly special. Once you try this, you will have a hard time going back to your original recipe.

Yield: 12–15 latkes • meat

3	large potatoes
1	small onion
2	eggs
1 tsp	salt
¼ cup	matzah meal
2 Tbsp	mayonnaise
1½ Tbsp	mustard
6 Tbsp	duck sauce
9 oz	pastrami or corned beef, cubed
	Oil for frying

1. In a food processor or in a bowl using a hand grater, shred potatoes and onion.

2. In a large bowl, beat eggs. Add salt and matzah meal. Add the grated potatoes and onion.

3. In a separate bowl, combine mayonnaise, mustard, and duck sauce. Add cubed meat and mix well.

4. In a frying pan, heat oil over medium-high heat. Place an overflowing Tbsp of potato batter into the frying pan. Place a Tbsp of meat mixture above it. Then place another Tbsp of potato batter to cover the meat mixture. Fry until the bottom is browned (about 4 minutes). Flip over and fry until the other side is also browned. Repeat for the rest of the latkes.

5. Line a plate with paper towels. Remove latkes from frying pan and place on the plate to drain.

Recipe by
Tova Lowenthal

Styling and photography by
Faigy Murray

Esrog-Infused Biscotti

Growing up, saving our esrog to bake something for Tu B'Shevat was always a big deal. Here is a delicious version of biscotti with a tangy esrog flavor.

Yield: 3 dozen • pareve

BISCOTTI

2	eggs
½ cup	oil
1⅓ cups	sugar
¼ tsp	salt
2 Tbsp	lemon juice
½ Tbsp	baking powder
2½ cups	flour
	Zest of 1 esrog
1 Tbsp	poppy seeds (optional)

GLAZE

1⅓ cups	confectioners' sugar
1 Tbsp	lemon juice
1 Tbsp	water
1 Tbsp	oil

tip

For a lemon-poppy twist, add 1 Tbsp poppy seeds to the glaze.

1. **Preheat** oven to 350°F.

2. **In** a mixing bowl, combine first 5 ingredients. Add dry ingredients, mixing until well incorporated.

3. **Divide** into 2 loaves. Spread each log on a baking sheet, making them about 3 inches wide. Bake for 30 minutes.

4. **Let** biscotti cool. Slice into ½-inch slices.

5. **Lower** oven temperature to 325°F. Return biscotti to oven and toast each side for 5 minutes.

6. **In** a small bowl, combine glaze ingredients. Lightly drizzle over biscotti.

Recipe by
Bracha Waintman

Styling and photography by
Chay Berger

tu b'shevat

Dried Fruit Pot Roast

The idea of combining dried fruit and meat was unappealing to me at first. But I tried it anyway, just for Tu B'Shevat. In the end, this meat came out amazing—I am definitely adding it to my favorites list!

Yield: 6–8 servings • meat

1	onion, diced
2 lb	chuck roast
	Salt to taste
	Black pepper to taste
1	garlic clove, crushed
1 tsp	allspice
2 Tbsp	red wine
1 cup	dried cherries
8–10	dried apricots

1. **Preheat** oven to 350°F.

2. **Place** diced onion on the bottom of a roasting pan. Place meat on top of onions and sprinkle salt and pepper. Rub in garlic very well and sprinkle allspice on top.

3. **Drizzle** wine over meat and place dried fruit around it.

4. **Cover** and bake for 1½ hours. Allow to cool before slicing.

Recipe, styling, and photography by
Faigy Murray

tu b'shevat

Fruit 'n' Greens Vinaigrette

Delicious flavor with minimal prep!

Yield: 6 servings • pareve

SALAD

1	ripe mango, cubed
1	avocado, cubed
¼ cup	dried cranberries
¼ cup	pomegranate arils
6 oz	spring mix or romaine lettuce

DRESSING

2 Tbsp	light olive oil
2 Tbsp	vinegar
3 Tbsp	sugar
1 Tbsp	water
⅛ tsp	salt

1. **In** a bowl, mix dressing ingredients until well combined.

2. **Place** salad ingredients in a large bowl. Add dressing and toss just before serving.

Recipe by
Bracha Waintman

Styling and photography by
Chay Berger

tu b'shevat

Pulled Beef Hamantasch Bites

Finger foods are always welcome at a Purim seudah—they're easy to serve and simple to eat. These are good at any temperature.

Yield: 24 hamantaschen • meat

2 Tbsp	oil
1	onion, sliced
1.5 lb	beef cheek
1 cup	beer
1 jar	Bone Suckin' Sauce
2 Tbsp	ketchup
2 Tbsp	brown sugar
1 Tbsp	mayonnaise
24	circles puff pastry dough
	Egg, for brushing

1. **In** a small frying pan, heat oil and sauté onions until golden. Place in a Crock-Pot with roast, beer, and sauce. Cook on high for 6 hours.

2. **Remove** from Crock-Pot, cool slightly, and shred with 2 forks.

3. **Preheat** oven to 375°F.

4. **In** a small bowl, combine ketchup, brown sugar, and mayonnaise. Spread on the center of each puff pastry round.

5. **Place** shredded beef on sauce. Fold into hamantaschen and brush with egg. Place on a baking sheet.

6. **Bake** for 15–20 minutes or until edges are golden.

Recipe by
Shaindy Siff

Styling and photography by
Chay Berger

Angel Hair Pasta with Wine-Infused Mushrooms

In this recipe, the garlic and wine combine really well with the mushrooms to form an elegant pasta dish.

Yield: 8–10 servings • pareve

1 box	angel hair pasta or spaghetti
	Oil, for drizzling
3 Tbsp	red cooking wine
4	garlic cloves, crushed
	Salt
	Black pepper
2 tsp	dried parsley
16 oz	small white button mushrooms

1. **Cook** pasta according to package directions. Once done, drizzle some oil over it to prevent clumping. Set aside.

2. **Preheat** oven to 400°F. Line a baking sheet with parchment paper.

3. **In** a bowl, mix wine, garlic, and spices. Toss with mushrooms. Spread mushrooms on baking sheet and bake for 40 minutes.

4. **Add** mushrooms to the pasta and toss.

5. **Serve** cold or at room temperature.

Recipe, styling, and photography by
Faigy Murray

purim

Sangria

This fruity sangria is a delicious treat—and a great way to use up all those mini flavored vodkas you get for mishloach manos.

Yield: 8 servings • pareve

1 large orange, thinly sliced

2 cups strawberries, quartered

1 lime, thinly sliced

11-oz can mandarin oranges in syrup (reserve liquid)

1 green apple, diced

¼ cup sugar

½ cup vodka (any fruity ones)

750-ml bottle red wine

1. **Combine** all ingredients in a large pitcher. Mix until fully combined.

2. **Refrigerate** for at least 4 hours before serving.

Recipe by
Shaindy Siff

Styling and photography by
Chana Rivky Klein

Spiked Punch Granita

This is perfect for the Purim spirit! So refreshing, with a hint of alcohol in honor of the occasion.

Yield: 4 servings • pareve

8 oz Bartenura Rose

2 cups Ginger Ale

⅓ container store-bought rainbow sorbet, semi-defrosted

1. **Pour** all ingredients into a container and mix until sorbet is dissolved.

2. **Freeze** overnight. Note: it won't be completely frozen in the morning since alcohol does not freeze.

3. **When** ready to serve, scrape with a fork and serve in mini glassware. Spoon a drop of the liquid over the granita for more flavor. Serve immediately.

Recipe by
Chaya Ruchie Schwartz

Styling and photography by
Faigy Murray

Get-Rid-of-the-Candy Cookies

The name says it all! Here is a fun way to get rid of all of the junk lying around your house while entertaining the kids.

Yield: 30 cookies • pareve

2 sticks	margarine, at room temperature
1 cup	sugar
1 cup	brown sugar
1 tsp	vanilla sugar
2	large eggs
2½ cups	flour
1 tsp	baking soda
½ tsp	salt
2 cups	leftover Purim nosh such as loose, opened candy, chocolate bars, and wafer rolls

1. **Preheat** oven to 350°F. Line a baking sheet with parchment paper.

2. **In** the bowl of an electric mixer, beat margarine and sugars until combined. Add vanilla sugar and eggs and mix well. Add flour, baking soda, and salt and mix until just combined.

3. **With** the mixer on low speed, stir in the candy.

4. **Using** a cookie-dough scoop, form balls of dough. Place on baking sheet.

5. **Bake** for 10–12 minutes or until browning at the edges.

6. **Let** cool and harden.

Recipe by
Faigy Stein

Styling and photography by
Chana Rivky Klein

purim

Chocolate Mousse and Crunch Cups

These cups of decadent mousse can go straight into the freezer until you're ready to serve them.

Yield: 10 servings • pareve

MOUSSE

7 oz	good-quality chocolate
1 stick	margarine
2 tsp	vanilla sugar
7	egg whites
1½ cups	sugar

CRUNCH

1 stick	margarine, melted
2½ cups	almond flour
1¼ cups	coconut flakes
½ cup	finely chopped walnuts
¾ cup	brown sugar

1. **Melt** chocolate, margarine, and vanilla sugar. Set aside to cool.

2. **In** the bowl of an electric mixer, beat egg whites until frothy. Slowly add sugar and beat until stiff.

3. **Once** chocolate-margarine mixture is cooled, fold into egg whites and mix until incorporated.

4. **Preheat** oven to 350°F. Place crunch ingredients on a baking sheet and bake for 20 minutes, mixing several times during baking.

5. **Once** ready, assemble the mousse in cups. Place in the freezer for several hours.

6. **Serve** frozen.

Recipe by
Shaindy Siff

Styling and photography by
Chana Rivky Klein

pesach

Creamy Green Soup with Meatball "Croutons"

This is that one soup we all look forward to having when visiting our hometown. The "croutons" elevate it to a dish that can grace a Yom Tov or simcha table.

Yield: 8 servings • meat

SOUP

2 Tbsp	oil
1	large onion, diced
16-oz	bag asparagus tips and cuts
3	large potatoes, peeled and chopped
2	large zucchini, chopped
2	frozen garlic cubes or garlic cloves, crushed
8 cups	chicken broth
2–4 cups	water

MEATBALL CROUTONS

1 lb	lean ground beef
1	frozen garlic cube or garlic clove, crushed
1 tsp	salt
½ tsp	black pepper
2 Tbsp	potato starch

1. **Prepare the soup:** In an 8-qt stockpot over a high flame, heat oil and add onions. Sauté for 3–4 minutes, until translucent. Add remaining vegetables and sauté for 15–20 minutes, until they are slightly browned at the edges. Add broth and then water to cover the vegetables by 1 inch. Simmer on medium for 1½ hours. Blend with an immersion blender until smooth and creamy.

2. **Prepare the meatball croutons:** In a medium bowl, mix all ingredients until just combined. With wet hands, form grape-sized meatballs. Place on baking sheet and broil on high for 2–3 minutes per side, until a crispy crust forms.

3. **Top** each bowl of soup with 3–4 "croutons" immediately before serving.

tip

These meatball croutons are also a great crispy topping for salad.

Recipe by
Shaindel Steinberg

Styling and photography by
Faigy Murray

pesach

Breakfast Cheesecake

This a great Yom Tov-morning treat. Make these after you kasher your oven but before you start cooking. Otherwise, you'll never get to it—and that would be a shame!

Yield: 1 9-inch round pan • dairy

CRUST

1¾ cups	Pesach crumbs
¼ cup	sugar
1 stick	butter, melted

FILLING

3 8-oz	containers whipped cream cheese, at room temperature
3	eggs
1 cup	sugar
2 tsp	vanilla sugar

1. **Preheat** oven to 350°F.

2. **In** a bowl, combine crust ingredients. Press into pan.

3. **Using** a hand mixer, beat filling ingredients until combined. Pour over crust.

4. **Bake** for 35 minutes. Turn off the oven and open the door a bit. Leave cheesecake in the oven for 1 hour.

5. **Refrigerate** for up to 2 weeks.

Recipe by
Chaya Ruchie Schwartz

Styling and photography by
Chana Rivky Klein

Cinnamon Bun Cookies

These are soft, buttery, and bursting with cinnamon flavor. No one will believe they are kosher for Pesach!

Yield: 1 dozen • pareve

COOKIES

4 cups	almond flour
1 tsp	baking powder
2 sticks	margarine, at room temperature
1 cup	sugar
1	large egg
1 Tbsp	pareve milk
1 tsp	vanilla extract

FILLING

¼ cup	brown sugar
2 tsp	cinnamon
2 Tbsp	margarine, melted

GLAZE

1½ cups	confectioners' sugar
3 Tbsp	water

tip

If you don't use margarine on Pesach, you can freeze 1 cup of oil for 2 sticks. If you don't use almond flour, you can put almonds in a food processor and process with the S-blade for at least 10 minutes on high—the results are almost the same.

tip

This recipe can also be used to create chocolate bun cookies by using an oil-cocoa filling.

1. **Preheat** oven to 350°F.

2. **In** a large bowl, whisk together almond flour and baking powder.

3. **In** the bowl of an electric mixer, beat margarine and sugar until light and fluffy. Add egg, milk, and vanilla sugar and beat until combined. Add flour mixture and beat until fully incorporated.

4. **Divide** the dough in half. Roll out each half on parchment paper into a 9x10-inch rectangle, about ¼ inch thick.

5. **In** a small bowl, combine brown sugar and cinnamon. Brush rectangles with melted margarine and sprinkle with sugar-cinnamon mixture. Roll up each rectangle into a tight log.

6. **Refrigerate** for 30 minutes.

7. **Line** a baking sheet with parchment paper.

8. **Slice** dough into ½-inch-thick slices. Place slices 1 inch apart on baking sheet.

9. **Bake** for 12–15 minutes.

10. **In** a small bowl, combine glaze ingredients. Fill a Ziploc bag with glaze and snip off a corner. Drizzle glaze over cookies.

Recipe by
Faigy Stein

Styling and photography by
Chay Berger

Potato-Pastrami Roses

These roses are always a hit. Set them on a plate of kale for the full rose-garden look.

Yield: 12 roses • meat

4 potatoes

Salt

Black pepper

Garlic powder

1 Tbsp oil

3 6-oz packages sliced pastrami

1. **Preheat** oven to 400°F. Grease cupcake tins with oil spray.

2. **Using** a mandoline, slice potatoes as thinly as possible.

3. **In** a large bowl, combine potato slices, salt, pepper, garlic, and oil.

4. **Slice** each pastrami strip diagonally to create narrower strips. Lay out 4 of the strips, making sure the edges overlap. Add potato slices on top of the pastrami, one after the other. Gently roll up the pastrami to create a rose. Repeat with remaining strips.

5. **Transfer** roses to muffin tins. Bake covered for 45 minutes. Uncover and bake for an additional 20 minutes.

Recipe by
Shaindy Siff

Styling and photography by
Chana Rivky Klein

Banana Split Pie

This cake is perfect for banana split lovers.

Yield: 8 servings • pareve/dairy

CRUST

2 cups	flour
1 cup	brown sugar
⅓ cup	quick oats
¾ cup	oil

RAZZLE LAYER

1 cup	Rice Krispies
¼ cup	mini chocolate chips
½ cup	chopped peanuts (or peanut brittle)
2 cups	vanilla ice cream, softened

BANANA LAYER

2	bananas, sliced
½ cup	caramel spread

PEANUT BUTTER LAYER

½ cup	peanut butter
2 cups	vanilla ice cream, softened

GANACHE

½ cup	heavy cream
1 cup	chocolate chips

TOPPING

½ cup	chopped peanuts

1. **Prepare the crust:** Combine all ingredients to form a dough. Spray a 12-inch springform pan with oil spray. Pat mixture into pan. Bake at 350°F for 20 minutes or until edges start to turn golden. Allow to cool.

2. **Prepare the razzle layer:** Fold all toppings into softened ice cream and pour onto cooled crust. Freeze until firm.

3. **Prepare the banana layer:** Spread caramel on top of firm ice cream and top with banana slices.

4. **Prepare the peanut butter layer:** In the bowl of an electric mixer, mix ingredients together. Spread on top of banana layer and freeze until firm.

5. **Prepare the ganache:** Microwave heavy cream on high and mix in chips until smooth. Allow to cool, then pour over the pie and freeze.

6. **Top** with ½ cup chopped peanuts.

Recipe by
Nechama Norman

Styling and photography by
Esti Waldman

shavuos

Peanut Butter Trifle

I'm always down for peanut butter anything, and this one is amazing! Make one large trifle or a few small ones.

Yield: 12 3-oz Mason jars • dairy

CHOCOLATE CAKE

2 cups	sugar
1¾ cups	flour
¾ cup	cocoa
1½ tsp	baking powder
1½ tsp	baking soda
1 tsp	salt
2	eggs
1 cup	pareve milk
1 scant cup	boiling water
½ cup	oil
2 tsp	vanilla extract

PEANUT BUTTER CREAM

½ cup	peanut butter
8-oz	container cream cheese
⅓ cup	sugar
¼ cup	milk

Whipped cream

1. **Prepare Choclate Cake:** Preheat oven to 350°F. Grease and flour a 9x13-inch pan.

2. **In** a large bowl, combine the first 6 ingredients. Add the rest of the ingredients and mix well.

3. **Pour** batter into the prepared pan. Bake for 35 minutes.

4. **Prepare Peanut Butter Cream:** In a bowl, cream peanut butter, cream cheese, sugar, and milk. Transfer to a piping bag.

5. **Assemble:** Using your hands, gently crumble the chocolate cake—you want it crumbly but not too fine. Place crumbs in the jars. Pipe a layer of peanut butter cream over crumbs, then add another layer of cake, repeating several times.

6. **Top** with whipped cream and garnish with extra cake crumbs.

Recipe by
Shaindy Siff

Styling and photography by
Faigy Murray

shavuos

Cheesecake Bite Cookies

This innovative twist on dairy cookies is sure to be a success with your family and friends. The cookie serves as a crust for a cheesecake, and a delicious filling serves as the cheesecake part. A mini cheesecake in a cookie—yum!

Yield: 12–15 cookies • dairy

COOKIES

2 sticks	butter, at room temperature
1 cup	sugar
1 Tbsp	vanilla sugar
1	egg
2 tsp	baking powder
3 cups	flour

CHEESECAKE FILLING

2 8-oz	containers whipped cream cheese
3.5-oz	bar dark dairy chocolate, melted
3.5-oz	bar white dairy chocolate, melted
2 cups	confectioners' sugar

TOPPING

2 3.5-oz	bars dark dairy chocolate
2 3.5-oz	bars white dairy chocolate

1. **In** the bowl of an electric mixer, beat butter and sugar. Add vanilla sugar and eggs. Add baking powder and flour and mix until combined.

2. **Roll** out dough on parchment paper and form circles with a cookie cutter or overturned glass.

3. **Bake** at 350°F for 6–8 minutes. Allow to cool.

4. **In** a container or bowl, blend all filling ingredients using a hand blender. Place in the freezer to harden for 30 minutes.

5. **Using** a cookie-dough scoop, scoop out the filling and place 1 scoop on top of each cookie.

6. **Freeze** cookies.

7. **Melt** 2 bars dark chocolate and 1 bar white chocolate. Mix together to combine. Coat cookies in chocolate mixture.

8. **Melt** remaining bar of white chocolate. Drizzle over cookies.

Recipe by
Faigy Stein

Styling by
Atara Schechter

Photography by
Ruby Studios

shavuos

Cookies 'n' Cream Sandwich Bites

Each lil' bite explodes with refreshing, creamy flavor!

Yield: 28 sandwich bites • dairy

14	chocolate-flavored tea biscuits
1 cup	milk
23 oz (½ tub)	cookies 'n' cream ice cream
1 cup	chocolate chips
½ tsp	oil

1. **Prepare** 2 small loaf pans.

2. **Allow** ice cream to soften for 40 minutes.

3. **Pour** milk in a shallow bowl and place 7 biscuits inside for 15 seconds.

4. **Place** 3½ biscuits on the bottom of each pan. Cover with ice cream and level. Place remaining biscuits in milk for 15 seconds. Place wet biscuits on ice cream. Cover and freeze for 2 hours.

5. **Place** chocolate chips and oil in a microwave-safe bowl and heat for 1 minute. Stir until melted. Heat for longer if necessary.

6. **Remove** ice cream sandwich logs from freezer and place on parchment paper. Pour chocolate over logs and return to pans. Freeze to harden.

7. **Cut** into 1-inch squares. Allow to defrost 10 minutes before serving.

Recipe, styling, and photography by
Mirel Freylich

Mocha Cheese Bars

There's nothing like those indulgent Shavuos-morning treats (and cheats!).

Yield: 1 9x13-inch pan • dairy

BASE

1 stick plus	
2 Tbsp	butter, softened
2 cups	dark brown sugar, packed
2	eggs
2 Tbsp	coffee granules dissolved in
⅔ cup	boiling water
3 cups	flour
2 tsp	baking powder
½ tsp	baking soda
½ tsp	salt

CHEESE MIXTURE

8-oz	container cream cheese (not whipped)
1	egg
⅓ cup	sugar

ADD-INS (OPTIONAL)

Pillow Kliks

Chopped dairy chocolate—dark and white

Chopped pecans

Dairy chocolate chips

1. **Preheat** oven to 350°F.

2. **In** the bowl of an electric mixer, cream butter and sugar. Add eggs and coffee and mix until combined. Add dry ingredients and mix just until incorporated. Spread batter in a 9"x13" pan.

3. **Combine** cheese mixture ingredients. Drop spoonfuls of the cheese mixture on the batter.

4. **Bake** for 20 minutes.

5. **Remove** from oven and sprinkle add-ins on cake. You may need to gently press them in.

6. **Return** to oven for another 25 minutes or until set. Allow to cool.

7. **Cut** into bars.

Recipe by
Chaya Ruchie Schwartz

Styling and photography by
Chay Berger

shavuos

Suppertime

There may be ketchup splattered on the table and some chairs,

A dish might just have shattered hard when you were unawares,

The cutlery can clatter to the floor and disappear

Amid the lively chatter; still, it's music to your ears.

If every dish gets tasted—only tasted!—it's a thrill.

And sometimes food is basted with exhausted tears you spill.

The sauce is mostly pasted on cute faces, yes, but still,

There are no efforts wasted, as inside you are fulfilled.

Are things not as impressive as the picture on the page?

The scene in sight suggestive of a battle being waged?

Your cooking's not reflective of whatever is the rage?

It's *love* that makes things festive where it matters.

Here's your stage.

Q399

I make my own cocoa mix and use it the whole winter. You can tweak it to your taste.

DIY Hot Cocoa Mix

Ingredients:
1 1-lb can cocoa powder
2 1-lb boxes confectioners' sugar
1 container vanilla sugar
Generous pinch salt
1 cup powdered milk (optional)

Directions:
Mix all ingredients together and store in an airtight container. When ready to use, add hot milk or water.

Q439

My boys enjoy hot poppers from the local takeout places. Here's a homemade recipe.

Hot Poppers

Ingredients:
2 chicken cutlets
2 Tbsp* Frank's RedHot Sauce (original or buffalo)
1 Tbsp olive oil
1 tsp chili powder

Directions:
Preheat oven to 400°F.
Cut each chicken cutlet into 4–6 pieces. Put chicken and all ingredients into a 9-inch round pan. Mix to spread sauce evenly over chicken. Cover with foil and bake for 1 hour.
*Adjust amount of hot sauce to suit your taste.

Q407

People are always asking me for the recipe after tasting my cinnamon buns. Here it is…

Cinnamon Buns

Ingredients:
Dough:
2 Tbsp dry yeast
2 cups warm water
9 cups flour
1 cup sugar
1 cup oil
2 Tbsp vanilla sugar
3 eggs
Pinch salt

Filling:
2 cups sugar
3 Tbsp confectioners' sugar
2 Tbsp vanilla sugar
1 package instant vanilla pudding mix
3 Tbsp cinnamon

Oil, for brushing

Directions:
In a large bowl, dissolve yeast in water and let stand a few minutes until activated. Add remaining dough ingredients. Let rise for 1 hour. Take challah (without a *brachah*).
In a small bowl, mix all filling ingredients.
Preheat oven to 350°F. Line baking sheets with parchment paper.
Cut dough into 4 pieces. Roll out each piece into a rectangle and brush with oil. Cover with ¼ of the filling. Roll up the dough and slice it. Place slices on baking sheets.
Bake for 20 minutes.

Q448

Here is a recipe that's easy a

Mushroom-Cheese Q

Ingredients:
1 onion, diced
1 Tbsp oil
8 oz canned or fresh mushroo
½ cup cottage cheese
½ cup sour cream
2 eggs
Salt to taste
Black pepper to taste
1 unbaked pie shell
Shredded mozzarella cheese, sprinkling (optional)

Directions:
Preheat oven to 350°F.
In a frying pan, sauté onions in translucent. Add mushrooms a for about 10 minutes.
In a bowl, combine cottage che sour cream, and eggs. Add sa mushrooms and onions and sa pepper. Pour into unbaked pie sprinkle shredded mozzarella, for added cheesiness. Bake fo

Q606

Microwave Chocola Mug Cake

Ingredients:
¼ cup flour
¼ cup sugar
2 Tbsp cocoa
⅛ tsp baking soda
⅛ tsp salt
3 Tbsp milk or orange juice